Even the Best of Us

Even the Best of Us

Clergy Sexual Failure—
The Church's Hidden Sin

Dwight A. Perry and
Elizabeth O. Pierre

WIPF & STOCK · Eugene, Oregon

EVEN THE BEST OF US
Clergy Sexual Failure—The Church's Hidden Sin

Wipf & Stock
An Imprint of Wipf and Stock Publishers
199 W. 8th Ave., Suite 3
Eugene, OR 97401

www.wipfandstock.com

PAPERBACK ISBN: 978-1-7252-5170-0
HARDCOVER ISBN: 978-1-7252-5171-7
EBOOK ISBN: 978-1-7252-5172-4

02/08/22

All Scripture quotations, unless otherwise noted, are from the New American Standard Bible®, copyright © 1960, 1962, 1963, 1968, 1971, 1972, 1973, 1975, 1977, 1995 by The Lockman Foundation. Used by permission.

This book is dedicated to all the victims of sexual abuse by clergy. May the Church of Jesus Christ rise up and aggressively root out this hidden evil.

Contents

Acknowledgments | ix

Preface | xi

1. The Church Too Movement Is Unfortunately Too Late | 1
2. Who You Are Is Not What People See on Sunday | 8
3. Activity without Substance | 22
4. Just the Emotions, Ma'am; Just the Emotions, Ma'am | 35
5. Sex Is More than an Event; It Is a Relationship | 46
6. Pornography, the Hidden Evil | 56
7. The Unique Trauma of Clergy Sexual Misconduct | 70
8. Clergy Misconduct and Recovery | 79
9. Concluding Thoughts | 89

Bibliography | 93

Acknowledgments

In any work such as this there are so many people to thank. I want first of all to thank my coauthor, Dr. Elizabeth Pierre, who wrote chapters 7 and 8. She is a rising star in the field of theological education. As an old man, my days on this earth are coming to an end. However, if the Lord wills, she will have another thirty-plus years to influence the church and invest in the next generation of pastors and leaders to become more whole as they seek to minister to others. Secondly, I want to thank Wipf and Stock for taking a chance on a rather controversial subject such as clergy failure; the editorial and acquisition staff have been outstanding. Finally, I want to thank the love of my life, Dr. Cynthia Perry. By the time this book is published we will have been married for over forty-one years and for all but two months of that time she has also served in full-time ministry with me. I remember those early lean days—and I mean lean—when we prayed for our next meal and God provided. I love you, and I am so proud of you and the ministry that you have had to me and to literally thousands of others. May you continue to speak truth and be truth to so many. I am indeed a blessed man because of you.

Preface

SEVERAL YEARS AGO, ONE of my spiritual idols unfortunately fell into sexual sin, which I discuss further in chapter 1. I was disheartened, I was shocked, not so much that it had occurred to him, but by the fact that all of us, no matter how large or influential our ministry might be, can fall into sexual sin. As I write this preface, we are praying for Liberty University, the largest Christian university in the United States. Their president has resigned in scandal, and it reminds me again some 30-something years later that, yes, even for those of us who represent Christ as leaders in his church, sexual sin can befall "even the best of us." It is the prayer of my friend and colleague Dr. Elizabeth Pierre and myself that as you read this book, whether you are a clergy person or not, you will be gripped with the holy reality that "there but for the grace of God go I" and how utterly needy and dependent all of us are on him who is the King of kings and the Lord of lords.

1

The Church Too Movement Is
Unfortunately Too Late

As a person who is now in his mid-60s, I grew up during an era in America where the question that was being asked was whether we were no longer a society that valued religion as central to our existence but had moved into being a secular society, where going to church was no longer a normative experience but had become abnormal. Many pastors and theologians were asking the question, as we entered into the 1970s, is there a new way to do church that unbelievers would flock to? Then, out of nowhere, a young man by the name of Bill Hybels, who had been a youth pastor in a suburb of Chicago, decided to do something that at that time was totally radical. He decided to make church "unchurchy" and intentionally structure his church and his worship experiences around the unchurched. He came to the decisions he reached, as the folklore would tell us, by walking through his target community and asking his neighbors what they did not like about church. After gathering a great deal of input around this question, he structured his church to avoid the four of five things his unchurched neighbors said they hated. Almost immediately this youth group of teenagers and 20-somethings grew overnight and continued to grow so large that Pastor Bill and the young people around him had created a movement of churches known as "seeker-targeted" and "seeker-sensitive" congregations whose methodology was built around creating an open and warm environment, whether it be the worship, the preaching, or even where the services were held (in an old movie house), that unchurched people would gravitate to.[1]

Pastor Bill became an overnight success until one day almost forty years later it all came crashing down.

This church, which came to be known as Willow Creek Community Church, had grown to more than 25,000 people with several campuses. Pastor Bill was only a few months away from officially retiring as the church's senior pastor. His successors had been chosen, but it then became known that there were some serious accusations of a sexual nature against Pastor Bill, and not just one but an unraveling of several from various women over a period of several years. These accusations eventually led to the resignation of not only Pastor Bill, but his chosen successors and the elder team who had supervised Pastor Bill. A church that once was looked up to as the benchmark of effective ministry now was being seen as a place where an alleged predator was allowed to exist for several years.

When the Lord began to put on my heart the need for a book that looked at clergy failure several years ago, I did not know how relevant this topic would be today. There was no such thing as the Me Too movement,[2] let alone the "Church Too" movement.[3] Sexual failure on the part of the clergy was an established fact, but it was seen, at least by some of my evangelical brothers and sisters, as a thing that took place in the Catholic Church or among leaders

---

1. Hybels and Hybels, *Rediscovering Church*.

2. The Me Too movement is a movement against sexual harassment and sexual abuse where people publicize their allegations of sex crimes committed by powerful and/or prominent men. In 2006 Tanara Burke founded the Me Too movement using the phrase "me too" to raise awareness of the pervasiveness of sexual abuse and assault in society. The phrase developed into a broader movement following the 2017 use of #MeToo as a hashtag following the Harvey Weinstein sexual abuse allegations. https://en.wikipedia.org/wiki/Me_Too_movement.

3. FaithTrust Institute, "#MeToo #ChurchToo," https://www.faithtrustinstitute.org/churchtoo.

of the charismatic persuasion of the church here in America and not a problem among evangelicals as a whole. The years since this book first came into my heart and mind have proven this unfounded assumption wrong. Sexual failure on the part of clergy is unfortunately pervasive among all types of leaders of various faith traditions.

As I write these words, I am also so mindful of the wonderful and true phrase, "There but for the grace of God go I."[4] This is why I write this book along with my coauthor, Dr. Elizabeth Pierre, with a sense of utter dependency on the grace of God, knowing that only he is able to complete in me that which he began.[5]

Well, let's begin the journey . . .

Patrick Means, author of *Men's Secret Wars*, reports that 63 percent of pastors surveyed confirmed that they are struggling with sexual addiction or sexual compulsion including but not limited to the use of pornography, compulsive masturbation, or other secret sexual activity.[6]

In 2016 Josh McDowell commissioned in conjunction with Covenant Eyes, an online accountability tool, a major study by the Barna Research Group on pornography.[7] The study, which involved three thousand participants, including, adults, teenagers, and pastors, analyzed the effects of pornography on pastors, churches, the general population, and young people. Four hundred thirty-two pastors were included in the study and 338 youth pastors. Barna found that

> 57 percent of pastors and 64 percent of youth pastors admit they have struggled with porn either currently or in the past. Overall 21 percent of youth pastors and 14 percent of pastors admit they currently struggle with using porn.

---

4. Source unknown. Tradition has ascribed it to John Bradford (1510–555), the English evangelical preacher and martyr.

5. See Phil 1:6.

6. Means, "How Many Pastors," 29.

7. McDowell, *Porn Phenomenon*.

In comparison, 47 percent of men and 12 percent of women in general seek out porn at least once or twice a month. And about 27 percent of Christian men and 6 percent of Christian women actively look for porn within that period of time . . .

A solid majority of pastors currently using porn said that it negatively impacts their ministry (75% of youth pastors, and 64% of pastors), though twice as many youth pastors (44%) as pastors (18%) said that was "very true." . . .

Married women, too, are less likely to look for porn. Two percent of married Christian women look once or twice a month, compared to 9 percent of single women . . .[8]

Kathlyn Flynn in her book states that 76.5 percent of those surveyed said they knew a clergy colleague who had been sexually involved with a member of their congregation.[9] A 1998 study by J. W. Thoburn and J. O. Balswich found that among all professional helpers, clergy have the highest rate of sexual exploitation.[10] For years women have been reporting sexual abuse by trusted mentors and other leaders.

Carolyn Holderread Heggen, in her article "Sexual Abuse by Church Leaders and Healing for Victims," makes the following statement: "The language used to describe the sexual involvement of a church leader with someone under his care or influence has often distracted us from properly understanding and addressing the problem.[11]

"Marie Fortune, an early and prominent advocate for victims, emphasizes the need to correctly frame and name the problem.

It is neither appropriate nor helpful to see clergy sexual abuse as primarily an issue of deficient individual morality or to consider it an affair, a sexual relationship, or even adultery. These terms imply a mutuality and consent

8. Lee, "770 Pastors."

9. Flynn, *Sexual Abuse of Women*, 3.

10. Thoburn and Balswick, "Demographic Data."

11. Heggen, "Sexual Abuse by Church Leaders," 83.

that is lacking when a trusted leader becomes sexually involved with a parishioner; authentic consent requires an equality of power in a relationship. It is instead, abuse. Clergy sexual abuse occurs when one who is in a position of trust or power takes advantage of someone entrusted to his care. It is an egregious exploitation of power, a profound violation of professional ethics, and a repudiation of Christian love and care.[12]

Peter Rutter, author of *Sex in the Forbidden Zone: When Men in Power—Therapists, Doctors, Clergy, Teachers, and Others—Betray Women's Trust*, warns of sexual behavior or erotic expression or interest that occurs in the forbidden zone—namely, any professional relationship of trust and unequal power. Sexualized behaviors that are forbidden may or may not include actual physical touch. They may include unusual attention, including gifts, frequent social telephone calls, letters, private visits, or attempts to develop a "special" relationship.[13] In other words, sexual abuse is not ultimately about sex or even one's inner loneliness or the pressures of the ministry, but it is about power—having power over someone who has entrusted themselves to your care. This is always the responsibility of the professional, the person with the most power.

In *Finishing Well in Life and Ministry*, Bill Mills and Craig Parro share the following statistics.

- 1,500 pastors leave the ministry each month due to moral failure, spiritual burnout, or contention in their churches.

- 80 percent of pastors and 84 percent of their spouses feel unqualified and discouraged in their role as pastors.

- 50 percent are so discouraged that they would leave the ministry if they could, but have no other way of making a living.

---

12. Fortune, *Is Nothing Sacred?*, quoted in Heggen, "Sexual Abuse by Church Leaders," 83.

13. Rutter, *Forbidden Zone,* quoted in Heggen, "Sexual Abuse by Church Leaders," 3.

- 70 percent said the only time they spend studying the Word is when they are preparing their sermons.

- Almost 40 percent polled said they have had an extramarital affair since beginning their ministry.

- 80 percent of seminary and Bible school graduates who enter the ministry will leave the ministry within the first five years.

- 90 percent of pastors said their seminary or Bible school training did only a fair to poor job preparing them for ministry.[14]

What seems to be the common threads among all the stated research:

1. Pastoral departure is rampant.

2. Seminary and other forms of ministerial training do not seem to be enough.

3. Workaholism is common.

4. Sexual temptation and moral failure are common.

5. Discouragement and depression are common.

6. The majority of pastors feel their work negatively impacts their family.

> *Focus on the Family* has reported (http://www.parsonage.org/) that we in the United States lose a pastor a day because he seeks an immoral path instead of God's, seeking intimacy where it must not be found. F.O.F. statistics state that 70% of pastors do not have close personal friends, and no one in whom to confide. They also said about 35% of pastors personally deal with sexual sin. In addition, that 25% of pastors are divorced. The statistics I had with church growth resources is even higher. Pastors who tend to be very educated seem to have the ability to embark in sin on Saturday and preach the Word on Sunday without thinking anything is wrong.[15]

14. Mills and Parro, *Finishing Well*, 1.

15. Krejcir, "Statistics on Pastors," lines 107–15.

Conclusion

I have tried to establish in this first chapter a sense of urgency as it relates to the issue of clergy failure. One thing I do want to clarify is the fact that clergy misconduct is not simply limited to married pastors. There are many clergy who are single in ministry as well. They also have to be aware of the fact that all clergy, whether married or not, are open to misconduct. It is my hope that as both Dr. Pierre and I walk through this most painful of subjects, all who read this book will realize that "even the best of us" can succumb to the subtle lie of the enemy in the area of moral and sexual sin. It is also my hope, as we continue to have this conversation, chapter by chapter, that by the end of this book the reader will have a sense of renewed hope that God is still God and he is still calling his saints who are called to ministry to be a holy priesthood set apart for God.

Questions for Further Consideration

1. Out of the signs mentioned in chapter 1 that led to moral failure, which one or ones do you struggle with?

2. Respond to this statement: Sexual abuse is not ultimately about sex or even one's inner loneliness or the pressures of the ministry, but it is about power—having power over someone who has entrusted themselves to your care. Do you agree or disagree? Why?

3. Were you surprised by the statistics quoted related to clergy failure? What actions has the information shared in this chapter inspired you to make?

2

Who You Are Is Not
What People See on Sunday

As MINISTERS OF THE gospel, most of us have been trained to value
the outside more than the inside. Sure, we talk about prayer and
the importance of the inner life, but how many of us realize that we
spend more time in crisis situations or on outward ministry projects, like writing a book on clergy failure, than we do nurturing
our own souls? This tendency is reinforced by the fact that even
though we know and say that our inner life is important, we know
in reality we are not going to get paid based on how well our inner
life is doing, but on whether our sermon next Sunday morning
hits it out of the park again for the tenth week in a row. In my book
The Hole in My Soul, I talk about how, in each of our lives, all of us
have a hole that only God can fill. Depending on our background,
our family of origin, the trauma we have experienced either in our
past or present, that hole might be wider and broader and deeper
in some, yet it is always present.[1] For me, as a young man growing
up in the inner city of Chicago, my hole was the void of not having
a father for most of my growing up years. But even more than that,
it was coming out of an abusive home where I saw my father beat
up my mother at age six and with another woman at age seven.
This created in me a deep desire to please people, especially men,

1. Perry, *Hole in My Soul*, 14.

and to put my trust in what others thought of me and my performance. Growing up in the 1950s and 60s was tough enough, living
in a country that is so racially divisive, but starting life within the
context of such a dysfunctional home setting made matters even
worse. Thank God for my God-fearing grandparents, who took my
mother and her two sons (my brother and myself) and allowed us
to stay with them for seven years during our elementary school
years. My grandfather was a janitor who raised seven kids on a
janitor's salary and was one generation away from slavery, having
been born in 1900. He was a quiet man who worked the second
shift throughout my childhood and deferred to my grandmother,
who ran the house with an iron fist full of love. Out of this union
came seven children and 20 grandchildren, and even though we
lived in the inner city, the inner city did not live in us. I can still
remember my mother's words ringing in my ears: "Son, I don't
care if you are a garbage collector; I just want you to be the best
garbage collector there is." This philosophy of life started with my
grandparents, who lived during the very degrading time of segregation and Jim Crow and whose lives modeled this phrase that
all of us as grandchildren were exposed to: "In order for you, as a
Black person, to be considered excellent in this white, segregated,
racist world, you are going to need to be superior." Out of the 20
grandchildren, nine of us have either a PhD, MD, or JD, just from
this one little family. This is a wonderful testimony, however, it developed in me, especially with the deep hole in my soul, a perfor-
mance-orientated mentality that even to this day I have to watch. It
created in me, once I entered ministry, a workaholism that helped
me to become outwardly successful, but it almost fractured my relationship with my wife of now forty-one years. As I have matured
through the ups and downs of life and ministry, I have noticed that
this performance-oriented culture that I began to thrive outwardly
in was all around me both within the church and outside in the
broader society. What became important was not who you were
but what you did, and even more so how well you did it. This false
narrative is not only pervasive in the broader culture but within
the church as well, and is amplified even more within a church

culture that glamorizes success and gives enormous accolades to ministers who grow their church or ministries to significant size and influence.

Many years ago, our family was taking a well-deserved vacation. All of our kids were young and this preacher barely had two nickels to rub together but had scrapped up enough frequent-flyer miles, due to my multiple trips away from home when I worked on the national staff of my denomination, that we were able to fly to California for our long-awaited dream vacation. The kids were excited as we would be going to Disneyland and other California attractions, but as parents we said that we would do this trip on the one condition that we would visit the headquarters of the very popular ministry Focus on the Family (which has since moved to Colorado Springs). So we packed up the rental car and, in the midst of Disneyland and all the fun things, went to take a tour of the Focus on the Family headquarters. At the end of the tour, out of the clear blue sky, our tour guide asked if there was anyone who would like to see a live broadcast. This was not part of the tour, and so my wife and I (not too sure about the kids) were thrilled. They escorted us into a room where all we could see was an encased studio through some glass as we awaited the famous host of Focus of the Family, Dr. James Dobson. Finally, Dr. Dobson came in and right behind him was a couple that I did not recognize, but I did notice that the husband never let go of his wife's hand. The interview began, and I found out shortly that in the studio with Dr. Dobson was the well-known pastor and author Gordon McDonald, who had pastored the largest church in New England, had written one of my all-time favorite books, *Ordering Your Private World*, whom I had just heard within the last year or so at the Moody Pastors Conference, and who had stepped down as the president of Intervarsity Christian Fellowship due to a moral failure. I could tell that the couple was nervous by their body language. What I did not know is that this was the first public interview of this famous clergy couple, Gordon and Gail McDonald, since the fall had become public. As Dr. Dobson slowly and methodologically conducted the interview, it moved to a crescendo when he asked a question of Reverend McDonald. I can still hear the words even though it happened over 30 years ago: "Gordon, how did this happen? You are a best-selling author, the pastor of the largest church in New England, president of InterVarsity. How did you find yourself in this situation?" And with almost a quiver in his voice, in a whisper, Reverend McDonald said, "Jim, to be honest with you, I love my wife, but I was tired of trying to keep all the things going."[2] Being a young minister myself at the time, I will never forget that interview and how God in his sovereignty allowed me to experience such a profound moment that would shape my life and ministry.

Dr. McDonald by all outward appearances had everything that I was striving for: fame, a large ministry, family. But yet on the inside he was dying trying to live up to the expectations of others, which was also true of me as a young minister. He was giving more attention to the what was happening on the outside than on the inside and thus never really allowing God to deal with the hole in his soul.

In this chapter I want to focus on the inward journey of the leader. I am going to talk about some of the lies that drive us to be more outwardly focused than inwardly developed. I am going to look at the performance-oriented culture that we live in and how even as ministers we can be caught up in this driven, out-of-control culture. I am going to look at some of the root causes of why as leaders we allow ourselves to get caught up in this performance-oriented myth that places more worth on what I do than who I am in Christ.

The first root cause that I would like to explore is the use of the subtle lies of the enemy from within.

What are some of the lies the enemy of our soul seeks to feed us inwardly to hinder us from seeing that hole filled appropriately, and not inappropriately through sexual or moral failure in areas that God has never ordained for us?

Allow me to suggest four that have plagued me, though I am sure you will agree this list is far from exhaustive:

2. Focus on the Family, radio interview with Gordon and Gail McDonald, 1990.

Even the Best of Us

You are a failure; you will never be anything. This lie manifested itself in my life especially when I failed due to the perfectionistic leanings that I developed from childhood, where I was told in no uncertain terms, "I don't care what is happening in the world out there—in the Pulliam/Perry house, we are going to be successful." Or another way to say it: "In order for you to even be considered excellent as a Black man, you will need to be superior." This lie as I got older really manifested itself in my life when I did fail, especially at something related to the ministry. I would beat myself up worse than Muhammad Ali did in his prime against everyone he faced. This inner dread of failure also drove me to not be vulnerable to others and hindered me from forming the type of relationships that were not performance based.

Who you are is directly related to what you do. In an article titled "Five Reasons Pastors Are More Vulnerable to Sexual Temptation,"[3] Reverend Fisher gives five reasons why a pastor—if not careful—will fall into moral failure. With the first one I have been very careful to monitor:

A pastorate is a place of power—whether it be standing before people week in and week out declaring "Thus saith the Lord" or superintending a business meeting at church, the pastor/priest is seen as a position of both informal and, in many faith traditions, formal power. Within my own faith tradition, the African American church, we have a saying: "When the pastor speaks, God speaks."[4] Alexander Strauch's classic book *Biblical Eldership* writes that the twofold goal in writing his book was to "first help clarify the biblical doctrine of eldership and second, to help church eldership function more effectively."[5]

Ministers are often isolated and unaccountable for their actions. Because of the very public but also very private place of the role of clergy within a congregation, it is very easy not only to feel isolated, but also to operate with a sense of a lack of accountability. As I have analyzed the stories of clergy failure, even the story that

3. Fisher, "5 Reasons."
4. Black church colloquialism of unknown origin.
5. Strauch, *Biblical Eldership*, 11.

I begin this book with, the consistent theme is a lack of true accountability of the senior leader.

Protection and policies around ministers can be lax. Ministers are charged to administer spiritual and emotional care to their flock. The problem, however, in a dysfunctional congregational subsystem is an overreliance on the minister because of what they and typically only they can provide, coupled with overlooking the weaknesses in the life of the minister who provides these crucial areas of care for others.

Ministers have few people they can share their deepest struggles with. This is not only true for the clergy person but also for the pastor's spouse. Many years ago, my wife wrote an essay for our denomination entitled "Who Pastors the Pastor's Wife?" Her point in the short essay was to communicate within our denominational context the need for pastoral spouses to not only be affirmed in their call alongside their marriage partner, but also to realize the loneliness of that call and their need, similar to that of the pastor, to have someone with whom they can share the struggles of ministry. Pastoral spouses experience the "glass house syndrome"[6] with their minister spouse and their children.

Ministers frequently feed off the approval of others—they can be "approval addicts." Their identities can "revolve around the attention and comments of others."

> "A minister's wellbeing, if they are unhealthy, rises and falls with every 'good sermon' or 'sister Jones is mad at you.' Not only are broken church members looking for attention, but so are broken ministers," Fisher said.
>
> He adds, "Sexual tension in a minister/parishioner relationship is powerful and deadly. It pushes the button of an approval addict and the needy church member and can quickly lead to disaster."[7]

God does not love you when you fail, only when you achieve. In our performance-based culture, it is easy to enculturate this lie as everything we see or feel has a certain level of winners and losers.

6. Rainer, "Eight of the Most Significant Struggles," lines 11–13.

7. Fisher, "5 Reasons."

Every television show, every award show, every sporting event reinforces this fear. Even our conversations with other clergy can be laced with this underlying philosophy that what is valued are those ministries that seem to be successful based on the world's perspective of fame, size, and finances.

Your needs will not be met, so you must make sure you take care of yourself. For someone who is in ministry, this lie totally contradicts the very work that God has called us to do and diminishes the promises of God in our lives. In spite of this reality, it is still very true that for many in the ministry, because of the pressures of burnout, conflict, underfunding, and continual comparison to others who seem to be doing better, many clergy see a sexual affair as something they are entitled to as a means to fill that hole in their soul.

Second, not only does believing inwardly some of the subtle lies of the enemy lay a foundation for sexual and moral failure, the lack of understanding of the influence and impact of narcissism from the inside out contributes to sexual and moral failure in clergy. We need to build appropriate guardrails around our mind, which will impact our attitudes and our choices. This is especially important in our fallen world today, which is increasingly coming under the influence of our enemy, Satan, who seeks to infuse his lies in everything we do.

Dr. George Simon, in his blog post entitled "Functional Narcissism and Culture," writes about the development and impact of a culture that can be structured in a way that promotes—even rewards—narcissistic behavior. He goes on to say these words:

> We've historically seen narcissism as both an aberration and a disturbance or disorder of character. However, our culture of entitlement, permissiveness, and relativism has helped make it more the norm. Moreover, in far too many aspects of modern life, narcissism has actually become quite adaptive. When something is working, or at least appears to be working, there seems little reason to change things. You've heard the adage: "If it's not broken, don't fix it!" Folks who find their ways of seeing and doing things working for them and in so many ways

have little motivation to change course. So, while most folks think individuals with character disturbances *can't* change, the reality is that many times, and for so many reasons, they don't see sufficient reason to change.[8]

Before looking at the three areas in which this narcissistic mindset is fleshed out in the world we live in, we want to use a term that Dr. Simon uses, "functional narcissism," and see how it hinders relationships.[9] Because the narcissist is totally consumed with him- or herself, his or her ability to care for others is limited. Unfortunately for those who choose the ministerial vocation and are beset with functional narcissism, they are truly what the Bible calls "wolves in sheep clothing," or as the prophet Ezekiel would say, "wicked shepherds" (Ezek 34) who only care about themselves and not their flock. Simon has identified three places in our society where a culture of narcissism has grown and developed.

1. The workplace

2. Families

3. New Age development

If we are not careful, our workplaces, including the church for those of us who primarily serve in the church, can set up structures that feed into the leader and his or her vision so much that everything else is secondary. This is especially evident in ministries where the primary leader operates out of what Carolyn Weese in her book calls an "Icon syndrome,"[10] where everything in the church or ministry rises or falls on the impact of lack of impact of the leader. For example, if I were to ask some of you the name of Joel Osteen's church, many if not most of you could not (without Googling it, of course) come up with the name, but if I were to say Joel Osteen most of you would know immediately who I was talking about. Now do not misinterpret this last statement; I am not saying megachurches are inherently bad. As a matter of fact, some

8. Simon, "Functional Narcissism and Culture," lines 1–12.

9. Simon, "Functional Narcissism and Culture."

10. Weese and Crabtree, *Elephant in the Board Room*, 85.

of the most innovative ministry that is reaching the lost is housed in some of these large churches. However, what I am saying is we need to be careful to beware and discern the influence of narcissistic thinking in the workplace.

Second, narcissistic thinking can become foundational in our families if we are not aware of its subtle influence. In moving from an agrarian culture to a more urbanized culture, the centrality of the family in American life has taken on a totally different focus. Families, which were primarily seen as a means to produce goods and a livelihood, worked, lived, and grew up together, sometimes multiple generations in the same home. In the African American context, we have a saying that goes something like this: "It takes a village to raise a child."[11] Not only was this true a one hundred-plus years ago in a more agrarian-based culture, it was also true when I grew up in inner-city Chicago in the 1960s. For even though I did not have a father who for most of my childhood lived in my home, I still had my grandfather and mother, whom I grew up with along with scores of uncles and aunts and even non-relatives down the street, like Mr. and Mrs. Powell, who helped to raise me. Sacrifice for one another thus was normative, children had to work to gain special privileges, discipline was imposed—maybe sometimes too harshly, but it was imposed on all without favoritism. In reaction to a generation of scarcity (my grandfather's generation—the greatest, who lived through the Great Depression), and in reaction to my mother's generation, who were born, many of them, during the Great Depression, a baby boomer like myself, once he or she became of age, was engulfed by a post-World War culture and economy that taught us that family should be worshiped and that those things that maybe some of us as older boomers have gone through was not something we wanted our children to go through. We therefore swung, in my opinion, to the other extreme and deified the family to the point that we valued the things we could provide for our children more than the time we could spend with our children. This helped to contribute to a very narcissistic

11. African proverb that former First Lady Hillary Clinton used as the title of her book *It Takes a Village*, published in 1996. Origin is unknown.

environment where children felt they could get away with anything and accepted as normal practice a privileged experience.

Third, narcissistic thinking can manifest itself in the New Age emphasis of personal development as a right and not a privilege. From day one many of our children and grandchildren have been told that they deserve unlimited success, great health, and fabulous wealth, and if they do not have this and possess it with little cost, it is someone else's fault and not their own. This attitude has even filtered into the church. The question being asked today is not "Can I find a church where I can serve to use my gifts?" but quite the contrary: "Where is a church where I can do very little and have them meet my and my family's needs?" Such values as service, doing for others, and sacrifice for others over the last 30–40 years have been eroded so greatly that when we see them we hardly can believe them. For the minister who chooses, either wittingly or in some cases unwittingly, to fall into sexual sin, we need to do more work around how a narcissistic perspective influences some of the choices made that will lead a person down this dreadful path.

A third factor that influences how one's thinking can get twisted so much so that ungodly choices follow is not realizing the importance of developing, cultivating, and guarding one's own personal integrity. A person of integrity quite simply is one who says what they mean and means what they say. One of the issues in ministry is the lack of accountability many of us as ministers continue to enjoy. Unlike other professions where there is a person who is your supervisor, the minister might have a board of elders or leaders but, in terms of the day-to-day functions of their work, most senior ministers have broad discretion in how those duties flesh out and how they are done in terms of meeting a standard of quality. Besides that, the minister's time is typically self-regulated, which can allow a number of areas of temptation, including sexual failure, to come in. Loss of integrity does not occur overnight; typically it transpires over a period of time. Reverend Steven Koster, in his fine article "Why Pastors Have Affairs," reveals that sexual abuse among clergy is quite common. He cites one study that says "Clergy abuse is remarkably common—in one study, 12% percent of pastors admitted to having sex with a parishioner, and only 23% of victims ever reported misconduct to church officials."[12] His thesis in the article is that all of us need intimacy, but that pastors especially need to be careful to not cross appropriate intimacy boundaries in four major areas: physical, intellectual, emotional, and sexual. He talks about the importance of maintaining appropriate openings toward others, but not crossing clear boundaries of intimacy. This can become confusing at times for the person in ministry, whom the congregation looks to as someone with whom they can share their burdens, but the fact remains that the moment one begins to cross boundary lines, destruction and despair is right around the corner.

Koster then goes on to give some excellent suggestions on how to maintain appropriate boundaries, which I would like to quote in their entirety.

> The bigger question is how ministers can avoid intimacy developing where it does not belong. Here are some suggestions for preserving healthy boundaries.
>
> - Stay strong in your relationship with God. A minister who is more focused on personal leadership skills rather than on God's glory is walking into temptation. A pastor should not be arrogant, but remember they are but a fragile, broken tool in God's toolbox.
>
> - Cultivate healthy relationships at home that allow for all the doors of intimacy to be open. Invest at home first and foremost so you are strengthened for dealing with others. You can share the concerns on your heart without violating confidentiality. You can discuss feeling overwhelmed by the needs of the congregation without spelling out what each need is.
>
> - If your marriage is unhappy, get help, and get it now. Seek counseling in another town if necessary. Your marriage is for life, and it comes before your ministry. If your marriage falters, your ministry will crash.

12. Koster, "Why Pastors Have Affairs," lines 8–10.

- Likewise, congregations should demand pastors take time for family and time for your spouse. Your home is the foundation of your ministry—if it blows up, so does the witness of the church. The pastor should have support within his congregation to hold him accountable for preserving family time and avoiding burnout.

- Put safeguards on your interactions, especially with those of the opposite sex. Meet privately with a parishioner only a limited number of times before referring to a counselor. Avoid working alone with someone of the opposite sex—it is better to have multiple members of a team work together if possible. Make sure your office door has a window to allow greater accountability while still allowing for confidential conversation.

- Find a mentor or counselor with whom you can debrief on a regular basis. This is good for not only your marriage, but your ministry as a whole.

- Avoid sharing your personal challenges about your spouse with coworkers. This is a red flag for any marriage, a sign that emotional investments are being made in the wrong place. Find a mentor or counselor instead.

- Be aware of your emotional state, and consider explicitly how you are being intimate with others. The doors of intimacy reinforce one another. With whom are you intellectually or emotionally close at work? How will you manage the other doors? There are natural pressures on intimacy for pastors, which makes it all the more crucial you intentionally cultivate and protect them.[13]

One thing that has helped me in my own marriage down through the years is the truth, based on Luke 8:17 and Ephesians 5:7–16, that everything will be brought to the light either in this life or in the life to come. That includes every email, text, private message board, etc., because God loves us too much to let us simply stay in darkness.

13. Koster, "Why Pastors Have Affairs," lines 100–131.

Integrity or character, even though not necessarily seen, impacts how one lives. In the next chapter I will focus on how this critical component of character is developed through the fiery furnace of trials.

Conclusion

Who we are is not so much what people see, but what they do not see about us. The temptation, especially within the performance-based culture we live and work in, is to neglect the inward for the sake of the outward. Many years ago, as I was facing a crossroads in my own ministry and life, the Holy Spirit dropped into my life the little story of the two sisters Martha and Mary in Luke 10:38–42. The text reads as follows:

> Now as they were traveling along, He entered a village; and a woman named Martha welcomed Him into her home. She had a sister called Mary, who was seated at the Lord's feet, listening to His word. But Martha was distracted with all her preparations; and she came up *to Him* and said, "Lord, do You not care that my sister has left me to do all the serving alone? Then tell her to help me." But the Lord answered and said to her, "Martha, Martha, you are worried and bothered about so many things; but *only* one thing is necessary, for Mary has chosen the good part, which shall not be taken away from her." (emphasis added)

Notice, as some have claimed, that Jesus did not say Martha was a bad person because her focus was on service instead of Jesus; no he did not, but he did commend her sister Mary, who chose to keep her relationship with Jesus as her priority in spite of all that needed to get done. Why is this so critical? Quite simply because it is only as we continue to nurture and develop our inner self can we be persons who serve well outwardly—not in our power but Christ's power.

Questions for Further Consideration

1. What was your emotional reaction when you read the statement that most ministers care more about the outward vs. the inward as it relates to their personhood?

2. What role has the approval of others played in your life? To what extent has it influenced you? Why?

3. What insights did you take away from the section on narcissistic thinking? What impact has this type of thinking had on you personally and on your ministry? Are you willing to ask someone else this question and see how they would answer it?

4. Please write down or discuss with the person you are doing this study with what you learned about the importance of boundaries. Please write down or discuss with the same person what you might have learned when healthy boundaries were not established and maintained?

3

Activity without Substance

As I BEGIN TO write this chapter, I need to own up to the reality
that for the greater part of the last two days I have found myself
drowning in despair and weeping uncontrollably at times. My precious little granddaughter has gone through a traumatic medical
event where now we are facing the very real possibility that she
might lose most if not all of her hearing in one ear, with the dan-
ger of it impacting the other ear. I grew up without a father—no,
let me correct that: I grew up the first six years of my life with
an abusive, womanizing father who beat my mother continually
and with whom I had to intervene one time in our small little
kitchen , asking him to stop. Even before I put my trust in Christ
as a college sophomore at the University of Illinois, I wanted to
live and do much better than what I had seen in him as a husband and as a father. During the four years my wife and I dated,
we were never intimate sexually. Why? Because I wanted to do it
right. Children came along rather quickly for us, along with major
ministry leadership, so quickly that we found ourselves as senior
leaders in ministry with four children under eight. And I decided
then to devote myself to my children even in the midst of a growing ministry platform. Both myself and my wife—especially my
wife—sacrificed for those children, particularly as one of them was
a special needs child, with whom until this day we are still heavily
involved at their age of 38. When the grandchildren came, we were

ecstatic, and I became the typical spoil-my-grandchildren-rotten grandpa, so much so that my oldest son and his wife, who have three of our grandchildren, had to in all seriousness call and put me on a "time out," telling me that they were trying to raise their children with Christian values and my excessive gift giving was not appreciated. Then came Demii. Demii was special for a couple of reasons. For one, she was our first granddaughter. My son and his wife have our three older grandchildren (all boys), whom we love dearly, but a little girl is just different—with all my degrees I still can't explain it. But I digress. Second, she is more like my daughter than my granddaughter, for we are extremely close and, yes, I do give her everything her eyes desire. Well what is the point of this story? Quite simply this: that even a man in his mid-60s as I am, who currently is serving as the provost of the most famous Bible college in the world, Moody Bible Institute in Chicago, is still being shaped in his character by the trials that our sovereign and I want to say good God allows in our lives.

The biblical author James would say it like this: "Consider it all joy, my brethren, when you encounter various trials, knowing that the testing of your faith produces endurance. And let endurance have its perfect result, so that you may be perfect and complete, lacking in nothing" (Jas 1:2–4). The word "tested" comes from a root word that is translated "proof" in this text, the Greek word *dokimion*, which can be defined as the means of proving, a criterion, a test by which anything is proved or tried, as faith by afflictions.[1]

What both James saying under the inspiration of the Holy Spirit is that God, who is sovereign, does allow trials in our life to test, to prove our faith so that, as it says in James 1:4, we might be mature in our faith (perfect, complete—*teleios*).[2] The image is of fully complete growth as compared to a child. Why? So that we might grow in wisdom (James 1:5–8), knowing that God is a God who graciously will give to the one who asks in faith all that they need as a fully complete, mature child of the King. I don't know about you, but I like the wisdom part of this text. I like the being

1. Zodhiates, *Hebrew-Greek Key*, 1383.
2. Zodhiates, *Hebrew-Greek Key*, 5046.

so close to God that my faith can stand, as Paul says in Ephesians 6:13, in that "evil day" that all of us will face. Whether it is the evil day of illness, the evil day of the loss of a loved one, or even the evil day of a grandchild who has done nothing but be born into this sin-filled, fallen world and who possibly faces a life of silence from the outside, your faith can stand. Whatever your evil day is, whether you brought it on yourself, others have enacted it upon you unjustly, or God in his sovereignty, as in the case of the man born blind in John 9:2–3, when the disciples asked the question who sinned, either this man or his parents, Jesus would say, "It is neither that this man sinned, nor his parents; but it was so that the works of God might be displayed in him," your faith can stand.

Over forty years ago, I was going through one of the most difficult periods in my life. I had been fired unjustly from my first full-time vocational ministry call. I was newly married and my wife had gotten pregnant four months after we were married, so I had a child on the way. Not only was I fired unjustly, but the predominately white organization that had terminated me had begun to slander my reputation. As a young African American minister who had chosen to join this white conservative evangelical group as one of the first, if not the first, full-time African American staff persons, I was stunned, and even more so when after promising to extend our benefits so that our health insurance could be covered they reneged on that promise. Humiliated, broke, and broken, I was at a point of despair, especially since the initial conflict that led this action was not between me and my supervisor but between my supervisor and another of the African American leaders I had brought into the organization, whom I had discipled and whom I was simply trying to defend. One day, as I was in my study (don't be impressed; it was an enclosed porch in the two-bedroom apartment that we shared with some various and sundry four-legged creatures), my wife was prompted to share with me a passage from Scripture that not only encouraged me, but literally changed my life: Genesis 50:15–21, the story of a man named Joseph.

> When Joseph's brothers saw that their father was dead, they said, "What if Joseph bears a grudge against us and

pays us back in full for all the wrong which we did to him!" So, they sent a message to Joseph, saying, "Your father charged before he died, saying, 'Thus you shall say to Joseph, "Please forgive, I beg you, the transgression of your brothers and their sin, for they did you wrong."' And now, please forgive the transgression of the servants of the God of your father." And Joseph wept when they spoke to him. Then his brothers also came and fell down before him and said, "Behold, we are your servants." But Joseph said to them, "Do not be afraid, for am I in God's place? As for you, you meant evil against me, but God meant it for good in order to bring about this present result, to preserve many people alive. So therefore, do not be afraid; I will provide for you and your little ones." So, he comforted them and spoke kindly to them.

We do not have time to go into the full story of what happened, which began all the way back in Genesis 37, when Joseph, as the youngest of Israel's sons at 17 and the favorite of his father, had a dream and told it to his father and brothers, that one day they would bow down to him. This infuriated his brothers so much that they decided to throw him into a pit to die, only to be rescued by his brother Reuben, who sold him into slavery, where he ended up as the chief overseer of a man name Potiphar, as Genesis 39:2 says, "the Lord was with Joseph, and he was a successful man. And he was in the house of his master, the Egyptian. Now the master saw that the Lord was with him and how the Lord caused all that he did to prosper in his hand. So, Joseph found favor in his sight and became his personal servant; and he made him overseer over his house, and all that he owned he put in his charge." This was the first of three times during what I call the dreary stage that God would elevate Joseph in spite of his circumstance. Why? In spite of all the trials that Joseph went through, God was still with him and God's hand was upon him. Joseph would spend 13 years falsely accused, attempted to be killed by his own brothers, in one of the worst prisons of the day, and then, after serving faithfully with his one chance to get out, overlooked by the chief butler. Why? Because God, just like in our lives, was more concerned about Joseph's character than his comfort. Why? Because God, as in our lives, was more concerned about what was taking place on the inside of Joseph than about his outward gifts. Thus God must bring us to the end of ourselves before he can truly use us.

There are four lessons we can learn from the life of Joseph that will build a foundation for a life of purity in the pulpit whether we are married or single.

Lesson 1: Humility always precedes honor. Joseph was obviously a gifted person. He also was a privileged person. Genesis 37:3 talks about how Israel loved Joseph more than all of his children. However, what he had to learn, just like many of us have to learn, is that giftedness and personality are not enough; character and wisdom that come from hard times will always surpass giftedness.

Lesson 2: Our trust ultimately must be in God and not in our abilities. One of the patterns you will find as you study the literature in regard to pastoral failure in the moral and sexual areas is how this devastating behavior can happen, and a lot of times does happen, even among some of our more gifted ministers. The writer of Proverbs would say it like this: "Pride goes before destruction, and a haughty spirit before stumbling. It is better to be humble in spirit with the lowly, than to divide the spoil with the proud" (Prov 16:18).

Lesson 3: God's timing in our lives is almost never our timing. Just this morning, in trying to grapple with what is taking place with my granddaughter, the Holy Spirit put his gentle hand on my shoulder and told me to read Romans 8:28, which says that "God causes all things to work together for good [notice it does not say that all things are good] for those who love God, to those who are called according to His purpose."

Lesson 4: God must first work in us before he can work through us. This is the pain of the cross. Galatians 2:20 says, "I have been crucified with Christ; and it is no longer I who live, but Christ lives in me; and the life which I now live in the flesh I live by faith in the Son of God, who loved me and gave Himself up for me." In other words, God must crush me before he can use me.

While studying for my Ph.D. at Trinity Evangelical Seminary, I came across in one of my classes the work of the late Dr. James

Fowler. Dr. Fowler Ph.D. Harvard University in Religion and Society was a graduate of Duke University and Drew Theological Seminary. He taught at Harvard Divinity School and Boston College
prior to joining the faculty of Emory's Candler School of Theology
where he would eventually be named in 1987 the Charles Howard
Candler Professor of Theology and Human Development. Staying
at Emory until his passing serving from 1994-2005 as the full-time
director of the Center of Ethics at Emory. Closely related to the
area of character development is one's faith development. James
Fowler in his seminal work describes six stages of faith development. These stages begin when a person is in preschool and begins
to develop a basic concept of who God is from their parents and
society, progresses to a place where as a young adult, one begins to
internalize one's own faith by examining critically one's faith even
to the place in some cases of becoming disillusioned to a place of
maturation in one's faith, according to Fowler few people reach
this last stage where they live their lives in service to others without any doubts or reservations.[3]

Similar to the Joseph paradigm of four stages of development—the Dream Stage, the Dreary Stage, the Deliverance Stage,
and the Dynamic Stage—Fowler's faith development theory helps
us to understand the importance of transformation in the life of a
leader as a process which cannot and should not be short-circuit-
ed. Even though initial faith for many does take place during stage
2; development of one's own faith tends to take place toward the
end of stage three and into stage 4. It is during stage 4 that the faith
of our fathers and mothers either becomes our faith or we reject
it as their faith. It is also during this stage that a person makes the
three most critical decisions they will make in their life: who is
their master, what is their mission, and whether and whom they
will marry. Similar to the Joseph syndrome, it is during this very
critical phase that many will begin to pursue formal training or a
formal process toward ministry without having some of the inward character issues brought to the surface, substituting ministry

3. "James Fowler's Stages of Faith," http://psychologycharts.com/james-
fowler-stages-of-faith.html.

for the hole that they find in their soul and the acclaim of others as a substitute for the still, small voice of God. It is also during this very important formational period that places of theological training and education can unknowingly substitute, especially in the Western system of training, intellectual knowledge for preparation for ministry and totally miss the need for spiritual and character formation. As a practical theologian who has been teaching preaching and leadership for a quarter of a century, I completely agree that we do need to better equip our aspiring ministers in the application of good theology within their particular local ministry context, however, the foundation of this very important work is what has been developed on the inside. This is where the enemy of our souls is able to come in through the backdoor of unresolved issues (or even issues we are unaware of) and cause destruction. Gary McIntosh and Sam Rima, many years ago in their book *Overcoming the Dark Side of Leadership: How to Become an Effective Leader by Confronting Potential Failures*, described the characteristics of five types of leaders and the problems they are most likely to develop if their particular dysfunctions develop unrestrained.[4] Allow me quoting extensively from MacIntosh and Rima's book to give you an overview of each.

First, we have the compulsive leader:

> When our drive to achieve, fueled by unmet needs (such as the need for approval) is channeled in the right direction, it can be a power for good. However, when the need-fueled drive becomes misdirected, it can result in disaster as we have seen. The key that will determine whether we experience success or failure is the degree to which we become acquainted with our dark side and put in place the defenses that will prevent it from running rampant and trampling our ability to lead effectively.[5]

Pierre Bergeron in his article "The Compulsive Leader" states:

---

4. Bergeron, "Compulsive Leader," lines 1–6.

5. McIntosh and Rima, as quoted in Bergeron, "Compulsive Leader," lines 13–26.

The compulsive leader needs to maintain control at all cost. Because compulsive leadership results from the leader's own compulsive personality, the leader sees the organization as another area of his life that must be controlled. The leader sees the organization's or church's performance as a direct reflection of his or her own person and performance. He or she pursues perfection to an extreme, both in personal and organizational life. Compulsive leaders have a tendency to be very rigid and highly systematized their daily routine that they MUST follow meticulously. They will systematize exercise, devotions, work schedule and even fun things like family holidays.

Compulsive leaders tend to be very status conscious, look for reassurance and approval of authority figures, excessively devoted to work, often become workaholics and leave little room for spontaneity. Although compulsive leaders are on the "out-side," pictures of absolute order as far as grooming, clothing, speech, family and their work environment, on the inside, they are emotional powder kegs. They struggle with a heart that is angry, rebellious and believe that it is wrong to express their true feelings. These feelings can be the result a rigid childhood where unrealistic expectations were placed on them or childhood trauma to which they were not allowed to give appropriate expression. This is why it is common for such persons' repressed anger to be expressed in sudden and violent outburst, only to be just as quickly controlled, with appropriate apologies.[6]

Bergeron in his article on the narcissistic leader says:

It's a known fact that narcissistic leaders have an over-inflated sense of their importance and see the world revolving on the axis of "self." Narcissistic leaders use others to always "look good." After all, they're convinced that without their leadership, the organization or church they lead cannot reach its full potential. This often results in self-promotion and "exploiting," taking advantage of others in order to fulfill their own desires or

---

6. Bergeron, "Compulsive Leader."

self-aggrandizement. However, in spite of their tremendous drive to achieve significance, their restless ambition is rarely satisfied. I've met such leaders in my civilian ministry and military career. But behind the aura, lies at the heart of a narcissistic leader self-absorption and uncertainty due to deep feelings of inferiority.[7]

Narcissistic leaders can drive an organization into the ground with an overinflated sense of self-importance. They are very egocentric, almost to the point of not really even being aware of some of basic issues that are being denied all around them.

A third type of leader, who when unchecked causes problems to any organization or church, is called the paranoid leader.

Driven by strong feelings of insecurity and a lack of confidence, these leaders are afraid of anything or anyone, whether real of "imagined," that they perceive to be undermining their leadership. They are hypersensitive to how people act and react. They fear "potential" rebellions and that "someone" will try to overthrow their authority and take their place. They are highly suspicious, hostile and guarded in their relationships whether with colleagues and/or family members.

"Because they are deeply insecure in their own abilities, paranoid leaders are pathologically jealous of other gifted people," so they lead by dominating others rather than empowering. They easily create rigid structures and processes to "control" their organizations and/ or churches and limit the autonomy of participants and emerging leaders.

Paranoid church leaders have a tendency to see the church board as their adversary rather than an asset consisting of gifted leaders that should be assisting in leading the congregation.[8]

Paranoid leaders are prone to jealously and are deeply flawed as it relates to others. Due to their paranoid tendencies, it is hard

---

7. Bergeron, "Narcissistic Leader," lines 3–9.

8. Bergeron, "Paranoid Leader," lines 2–12.

for them to fully trust and empower others as they are always afraid of losing something: status, power, money, etc.

Codependent leaders tend to have been raised in environments where the rules of life where strictly reinforced and thus a person is never given the freedom to exercise their God-given passions and gifting. These environments are characterized by a controlling older person who exerts there will on everything in the family. This is one of the reasons codependent leaders gravitate to the church, especially the institutional church with its rules and regulations. They also get their self-esteem needs met by pleasing those in authority and acquiescing to their desires even above their own. Finally, codependent leaders have a hard time confronting others. They tend to look for the way of least resistance.

Finally, Bergeron introduces the passive aggressive leader:

> The passive-aggressive leader is a pessimistic individual who complains and procrastinates because her/she is reluctant to perform. This individual is the "resister" in a group and is intentionally inefficient. The origin of this reluctance is from two forces that are at oppressing ends. These are, the fear of failure and the fear of success that will lead to higher expectations that could eventually lead to failure sometime in the future.
>
> Although some passive-aggressive persons may enjoy the prestige of leadership positions, they dread assuming any form of responsibility. So "others" are always "responsible" for failure or when things go wrong. Because of the inner battle in their dark-side, passive-aggressive individuals are known for their outburst of intense emotions such anger and frustration. Exhibiting irritability and impatience behavior patterns, they can be verbally abusive and act in manners that are socially and professionally unacceptable when things don't go as they desire. This impulsive behavior is often followed by short-lived periods of sorrow and repentance. So, as you have guessed, colleagues are uncomfortable around such people and have a tendency to try to avoid direct contact and protect themselves from the next outburst.

The classical biblical character of a passive-aggressive leader is Jonah. Frustrated with God's call on his life, he decides to flee. He finds himself in a huge storm and his vessel is sinking. He is "forced" to confess that he is running from God and ends up overboard. It was only when he found himself in the belly of a giant fish that he experiences sorrow and repentance, however, not for long.[9]

In my own journey, I tend to gravitate toward the compulsive leadership style. Because of the hole in my soul that was developed during the time I was as a child in a very physically and emotionally abusive home, when I desperately desired the love and approval of my father, I became the classic overachieving person. Not all of this tendency was due to the home I was raised in for the first seven years of my life; I also grew up in an era in this country in the 1950s and 60s where in order for an African American to be considered excellent, he or she had to be superior. That's right, the computer did not skip over some words. In order to be perceived as excellent, if you were an African American you had to be perceived as superior. This context, within my home, within my soul, and within the broader society, created in me a compulsiveness that valued what people saw more than what I saw on the inside and even, after I trusted Christ as my Savior as a sophomore in college, what God saw.

This desire to please others, which, when balanced with not putting one's identity into what another person thinks or feels about you, which is good, but becomes destructive when our identity as a person is wrapped up in how others see us, can if one is not careful lead a person to not exercise appropriate boundaries. This is especially true for those of us who have been called to caregiving occupations: clergy, nurses, doctors, teachers, etc. Overcommitting not only our time but also our emotional and spiritual resources, as I described in chapter 2 with the story of Dr. MacDonald, brings us into a vulnerable place where we do not have the spiritual reserves to discern, as Ephesians 6 teaches us, the onslaught of the enemy and his many schemes. Similar to Martha in the Luke account, it

9. Bergeron, "Passive Aggressive Leader," lines 5–19.

also leaves us distracted with what many would call a good thing, service for Jesus, and miss out on the best thing, time alone with Jesus. This makes us vulnerable to the subtle attacks of the enemy, including crossing boundaries sexually with someone who is not our spouse, even though we are in the trusted position of being a clergy person. Failing to be strong in the Lord and in the strength of his might, failure to put on the full armor of God in order that we might be able to stand firm against the schemes of the enemy.[10]

Allow me to close this chapter on the importance of substance even above activity by quoting from Steve Koster's article "Why Pastors Have Affairs: Sacred Boundaries and Sexual Abuse."

> Physically, a pastoral role constantly calls for some level of physical presence. It might be a hand on shoulder during prayer, or a closed door for private confession and conversation, or even just being a leader who stands in front of people and is constantly seen. Being physically present is an important part of spiritual care. But, escalating physical privacy or finding excuses to spend time with someone who is already intellectually or emotionally close should be a major warning sign that a relationship is becoming inappropriately intimate.
>
> Serially abusive pastors may start with apparent emotional vulnerability and then escalate slowly to increasing physical interactions, often with apologies and prayers even as they continue to push sexual boundaries that should be sacred to their office.[11]

Conclusion

Who you and I are on the inside will ultimately determine what others see on the outside. Life, pressure, and unforeseen trials don't make us behave a certain way; they only bring out what was already inside that has not be touched by the grace of God. As Christ followers, and for those of you who are clergy, do not be

10. See Eph 6:10–12.
11. Koster, "Why Pastors Have Affairs," lines 73–85.

deceived: whatsoever a man sows he will reap (Gal 6:7–8). Activity without substance will always, especially in the pressures of life, lead to decisions that will bring dishonor to ourselves, our God, and the ministry that we have been called to serve.

Questions for Further Consideration

1. As you studied Joseph's story what parallels if any to your own story did you see?

2. Where would you place yourself on Joseph's stages of development and why?

3. Bergeron describes several types of dysfunctional leadership. Do you see yourself in any of these descriptions? Are you willing to share Bergeron's definitions with a spouse, close friend, work colleague and ask them if they see you in any of these descriptions?

4

Just the Emotions, Ma'am;
Just the Emotions, Ma'am

ONE OF MY FAVORITE shows growing up was a show by the name of *Dragnet*. (Shows you how old I am—the show was popular in the 1950s and early 60s). The lead character, Sergeant Joe Friday, was the strong, no-nonsense policeman who when investigating a case would often say, "Just the facts." This phrase was used by the producers of the show to communicate the image of an unemotional, non-subjective policeman who would not allow his emotions to get in the way and would be dogged in simply following the facts.

Growing up as a young man in a conservative white evangelical setting, I was taught that emotions, and specifically emotionalism, were bad. The particular ministry that had done so much to nurture my faith had, on the other hand, influenced me so strongly in the perspective that emotions obviously were inaccurate and thus could lead you astray if not strongly suppressed, that as I grew in my faith, I distanced myself from my very own racial and ethnic background, which had endured the blight of slavery, Jim Crow, and busing only to find itself in the 1960s on the edge of another civil war, the civil rights wars of the 1950s and 60s.

As I have matured in my faith now over these many years, I have come to what I believe is more balanced perspective: that God has given us the capacity to feel as a means by which we can begin to sense if something is off in our relationship with God and others. In other words, it is not a map, but a barometer as to what might be taking place underneath the surface.

In this chapter, we will explore the following themes:

- What is the role of emotions in humankind?

- What is trauma and what role does trauma play in the development of a healthy or unhealthy self-worth?

- What impact did the fall have on our emotions?

- The role of satanic accusations and how to defeat them.

- A brief discussion of the *imago Dei* and what role emotions played prior to the fall.

Let's begin with the role of emotions in humankind. Emotions are intense, short-term physiological, behavioral, and psychological reactions that prepare us to respond. There are three components to understanding emotions:

1. A subjective component (how you experience the emotion)

2. A physiological component (how your body reacts to the emotion)

3. An expressive component (how you behave in response to the emotion)[1]

How an individual experiences emotion is influenced by a person's family of origin, by their cultural and racial context, by early trauma they have experienced, and by reinforced norms and values conveyed by those a person interacts with.

Richard Plass and James Cofield address the role of emotion and illustrate the impact of one's family of origin as it relates to emotional development:

> Our individual relational reality was born of the connection of our parents. Without the loving and nurturing of others after birth, we would not have survived. The

1. Cherry, "Purpose of Our Emotions," lines 6–9.

relationships in our family of origin shaped and molded our lives. As we grew into adulthood, our relationships influenced the state of our souls for good or for ill.[2]

In their article "The Role of the Family Context in the Development of Emotional Regulation," Morris and colleagues suggest there is a direct relationship between a person's emotional development and their family of origin. They suggest three important ways this is manifested:

Firstly, children learn about emotional regulation through *observation.*

Secondly, specific *parenting practices and behaviors* related to the socialization of emotion and the development of emotional regulation.

Thirdly, emotional regulation is affected by the *emotional climate of the family*, as reflected in the quality of the attachment relationship, styles of parenting, family expressiveness, and the emotional quality of the marital relationship.[3]

As a child who grew up until age seven in a domestically violent home, where I saw my father beat up my mother and I tried to intervene even though I was only six years of age, I can personally testify to the role that the emotional climate of the family played in my own experience. I grew up not only with a deep hole in my soul that I sought to fulfill by being a person that pleased others especially men to my detriment, I also grew up with an emotional deficit and substituted reflection and the hard work of inner inquiry with a performance-based mentality which allowed me to gain my sense of self-worth by how well I performed.[4]

Eisenberg and Morris[5] and others have come up with a definition of emotional regulation. Emotional regulation consists of internal and external processes involved in initiating, maintaining, and modulating the occurrence, intensity, and expression of emotions.

---

2. Plass and Cofield, *Relational Soul*, 12.

3. Morris et al., "Role of the Family Context," 361–88.

4. Perry, *Hole in my Soul*, 26.

5. Eisenberg and Morris, "Children's Emotion- Related Regulation."

In other words, unlike some Christian traditions teach, including the North American evangelical model, emotions are central to one's humanity and are developed or hindered from developing in a healthy way foundationally through one's family of origin. Bandura[6] has maintained for several decades that modeling is a key mechanism through which children learn behavior. In other words, the old adage "Do what I say and not what I do" is simply that: an old, unproven adage that is not rooted in truth.

This is why social referencing is so important, whether for a child or an adolescent. Social referencing is the process of looking to another person for information about how to respond, think, or feel about an environmental event or stimuli.[7] Prior to adolescence a child's primary frame of reference is the home and the family; as one moves into adolescence, their primary frame of reference becomes one's peers.

Specific parenting practices are also critical in the development of one's emotional life and the development of a healthy emotional adjustment into adulthood. They argue that parents who are responsive and warm typically display specific types of parental behaviors and have certain beliefs associated with emotion that affect children's emotional regulation.[8] As believers who are hopefully shaped by a biblical worldview, such attitudes as kindness, patience, forbearance, and proper discipline, out of a motivation of love and not anger, should pervade.[9] Unfortunately, in many families, even and at times especially Christian families, the acceptance and encouragement to express one's emotions is downplayed significantly due to a misunderstanding of Scripture and an imposition of false and misleading supposedly "Christian values" that are rooted more in a European-American cultural orientation that focused on production and children as a means of

---

6. Bandura, *Social Learning Theory*.

7. Morris et al., "Role of the Family Context," 6.

8. Morris et al., "Role of the Family Context," 8.

9. See Eph 6:1–4a.

productivity instead of the nurturing and development of a child's soul, which includes their emotional life.[10]

In the book *The Relational Soul*, Plass and Cofield use as a foundation attachment theory.[11] They talk about how critical the first five years of a child's life are, especially as it relates to emotional maturity and development. This type of emotional climate within the family unit allows children to be treated as valuable, having been created in the image of God. I also experienced this firsthand. As I have mentioned a few times in this book, I grew up until age seven in a physically and emotionally abusive home. It has taken me 60-something years to begin to come to grips with the impact that this type of home has had on me as an adult. I am convinced to this day that what saved me and my brother was that we moved into the home of our grandparents, who until I went off to high school provided along with my mother the type of loving but accountable environment that allowed both my brother and myself to eventually thrive. One of the areas that was so critical to this turnaround was the ability to freely express myself and not fear physical retribution. Discipline was present in this house, however. My grandmother, the primary disciplinarian in the house, was also a true servant to all. It was not unusual, especially around the holidays, to find literally 30, 40, or 50 people in her house, eating and laughing and telling stories to one another. I always looked forward to these family gatherings, for as a young child they gave me a sense that this house was a happy house full of joy and laughter and people who really cared about you and wanted to invest in you. In spite of this reality, it was not a home that provided space for a lot of deep sharing. We played together and spent time together, but our true focus was on what we needed to do, not who we needed to become. This experience, along with the trauma of growing up in an abusive home, created in me a fear of really opening up. Expression of emotion in my family, even though it was not said, was considered weak. For example, as a young man I did not have anyone in whom I could confide. The closest person was my

10. See Prov 22:6; Eph 6:4b; Deut 6:7.

11. Plass and Cofield, *Relational Soul*, ch. 2

Uncle Barry. He did talk with me and provided the space for me to talk back. However, his emphasis was not so much on the sharing, but ultimately what I needed to do or should do as a young man growing up in a racially segregated America. These interactions both inside and outside the home led me to become very private about my emotions.

A second critical component in terms of emotional development is the impact emotions have on a person's physiological self. My wife and I read books for our date night. We use these weekly times to not only connect on a relational and emotional level, but also to connect intellectually and spiritually. A book that we are in the midst of reading as I write this chapter is entitled *The Body Keeps the Score: Brain, Mind, and Body in the Healing of Trauma*. It was written by a medical doctor, Bessel Van der Kolk, and even though it is not a Christian book per se, it is extremely helpful in understanding how past trauma can and does influence current behavior. As a child of abuse, I am just now over the past few years beginning to understand the impact the domestic abuse I experienced as young child has had on me over these past 65-plus years. The thesis of the book is found in the prologue:

> How can people gain control over the residues of past trauma and return to being masters of their own ship? Talking, understanding, and human connections help, and drugs can dampen interactive alarm systems. But we will also see that the imprints from the past can be transformed by having physical experiences that directly contradict the helplessness, rage and collapse that are part of trauma, and thereby regaining self-mastery.[12]

In Van der Kolk's book, he demonstrates from his perspective as a physician with forty-plus years of experience in serving victims of trauma the direct tie between trauma and the impact it can have on a person physiologically. He begins the book with a story about Tom, whom he met in 1978 as a staff psychiatrist at the Boston Veterans Administration Clinic. Tom, a former Vietnam veteran who 10 years earlier had served our country as a marine,

12. Van der Kolk, *Body Keeps the Score*, prologue.

was a man who had spent the July Fourth weekend holed up in his downtown Boston law office drinking and looking at old photographs rather than being with his family. His nights were not any better as his sleep was constantly interrupted due to nightmares so horrible that he dreaded going to sleep and stayed up most nights drinking. At the end of the war, all Tom wanted to do was to put his time in the service behind and for many years it appeared he was able to successfully divest himself of the trauma he had experienced as he attended college, graduated from law school, and married his high school sweetheart. However, the demons that Tom had to face as a result of the trauma he experienced in Vietnam eventually won out, and not only did it begin to impact his physical health with the excessive drinking and lack of sleep, but it also impacted him emotionally as he was unable to find any real pleasure in life, feeling dead on the inside.[13]

Other results of unresolved trauma are:

- Difficulties with focusing and memory
- Sensory overload and filtering what matters from what doesn't
- Difficulty sleeping and relaxing
- Learning new information and changing behavior
- Cultivating a sense of confidence and personal agency
- Fear and anxiety around taking risks
- Fully accessing imagination and creativity
- Self-doubt and perfectionism
- Chronic fatigue and exhaustion
- Maintaining motivation and a sense of purpose.[14]

As a pastor for over forty years now, I have come to learn that how emotions are expressed is only the tip of the iceberg. Our reaction to these emotional responses thus needs to be measured and prayerful, lest the person who is expressing emotion,

---

13. Van der Kolk, *Body Keeps the Score*, 7–8.

14. Forte, "Body Keeps the Score . . . (Book Summary)," lines 12–21.

especially if it is negative, retreat even further back into themselves and put up a protective wall around themselves if our position is instinctively negative. As an African American church leader, I come out of Christian subculture that is full of emotion. When speaking to a predominately white audience, when I don't get a hearty amen to a point I will prod the audience by saying, "In my church, they would probably shout on that point." It is a joke, but it does reflect somewhat accurately part of the unique ethos of the African American church, which is more emotive in nature than most majority-culture churches. As a religious people born out of the turmoil of slavery, the middle passage from Africa, Jim Crow, and even to this day continued racial disparity, the Psalms and the narratives of the nation of Israel, the songs of the spirituals, and gospel music are thus special to us as a people because they tend to touch our souls emotionally and allow us, in the context of what we have labeled "call and response" preaching, to participate along with the preacher in the sermon.

Earlier in the chapter, I mentioned briefly the concept of attachment theory. I would like to explore this concept now a little deeper. Attachment theory in psychology originated with the seminal work of John Bowlby.[15] "In the 1930s John Bowlby worked as a psychiatrist in a Child Guidance Clinic in London, where he treated many emotionally disturbed children. This experience led Bowlby to consider the importance of the child's relationship with their mother in terms of their social, emotional, and cognitive development. Specifically, it shaped his belief about the link between early infant separations with the mother and later maladjustment."[16] Bowlby had five main points to his theory of attachment:

1. A child has an innate need to attach to one attachment figure.

2. A child should receive the continuous care of this single most important attachment figure for approximately the first two years of life.

15. Bowlby, "Nature of the Child's Tie."
16. McLeod, "Attachment Theory," lines 1–9.

3. The long-term consequences of maternal deprivation might include the following:

   - delinquency
   - reduced intelligence
   - increased aggression
   - depression
   - affectionless psychopathy

4. Robertson and Bowlby believed (1952) that short-term separation from an attachment figure can lead to distress.

5. The child's attachment relationship with their primary caregiver leads to the development of an internal working model.[17]

For many, we unfortunately forget that we live as fallen people in a fallen world with other fallen people. When God said in Genesis 1:26–27, "Let us create man in our image, male and female," we sometimes forget that this meant that not only did God give Adam and Eve a spirit that was without sin and could commune with God, God also gave them a soul (a mind, will and emotions) so that every human being could commune with him- or herself within the context of their relationship with God. Theologians call this the *imago Dei*, for it expresses the wonderful reality that, unlike all other creation and creatures, God made humankind in his divine image. Unfortunately, due to sin, that image, which is still present in every human being, was marred and his creation, including male and female, became scarred for the remainder of time on this earth. This scarring was not just physical or intellectual but it was emotional as well, creating right from the beginning an estrangement between people that was not in God's original design.[18] This estrangement would multiply as the generations would come to occupy this earth and would create sexual, physical, intellectual,

17. McLeod, "Attachment Theory."
18. See Gen 3.

and emotional wounds that would bring more pain into a world, that already due to the fall was destined for pain.

One area that is not discussed as much as it should be is the role of Satanic accusation and its influence in our emotions. Revelations 12:10 talks about how Satan is the "accuser of the brethren . . . he who accuses them before our God day and night." One of the areas he uses to accuse us in and through is our emotions. He realizes that, as people who have emotions, if he can get us to focus more on our faults instead of on a God who loves us in spite of our faults and who can help us to deal with our faults, we will forfeit all that we have in Christ (Eph 1:3–14) and live like paupers when we are really children of the king. This does not mean that we do not realize, as I mentioned earlier in this chapter, that we live in a fallen world, with fallen people who do fallen things, but what it does mean is that in spite of that reality, we can still rise above our failures because we have a God who is sovereign overall and has equipped us, through the ministry of his Holy Spirit and through the prayers and the fellowship of his people, to be more than conquerors through him who loves us. The problem, however, is not knowing how to take a stand, as the apostle Paul teaches us in Ephesians 6, against the onslaught of the enemy, especially in the "evil day" (v. 13), that time in our lives when everything seems crazy and out of control and the only thing we have to hold onto is the promises of God. This is where biblical accountability and spiritual covering is so very important. Knowing, as Paul says in 2 Corinthians 1:10–11, that I am in a community whose very "prayers will deliver me" gives me the strength to continue on despite what is taking place all around me and even inside of me.

Conclusion

Emotions are not something to be suppressed; they are God-given signposts to alert us to what might not be clearly seen is going wrong in our lives. We need to not rely upon them, but neither should we neglect them as they are used by God to bring us to the end of ourselves and thus help us to draw near to an almighty God.

Questions for Further Consideration

1. As you read the material on attachment theory what was your response? What insight into your own life were you able to gain as you read this material?

2. How have you seen trauma impact your own life and impact those whom you are seeking to minister to? What coping mechanisms do you have in place to appropriately deal with trauma?

3. What role does satanic accusation play in our emotional stability? How can we tell if our emotions are being manipulated by the schemes of the enemy or simply or by own fallen tendencies? What role does biblical accountability play in this discernment process?

5

Sex Is More than an Event;
It Is a Relationship

By the time this book is published, my wife and I will have cele-
brated forty-one years of marriage. Early in our marriage, I remember hearing this little phrase at a marriage conference we attended:
"Sex is more than an event; it is a relationship." The speaker would
go on to say, "Men, did you know that when you wake up in the
morning and speak kindly to your wife, you are having sex? Did
you know that when you clean the house, you are having sex, and
especially when you get up in the middle of the night to take care
of the crying baby, you are preparing your wife for sex? For, unlike men, who in general see sex primarily through the lens of the
act, women in general see sex through the lens of the relationship,
or the closeness, the intimacy of the act."[1] These words literally
changed my life. First, as someone who came to Christ as a young
adult some 47 years ago, I was raised within a Christian subculture
that did not put a lot of emphasis on relationships, but on the task
and call of doing the ministry. Second, this was already my bent
anyway, growing up in the 1950s and 1960s during the height of
the civil rights movement and the height of racial segregation in
this country when, as a young African American, I was taught that

1. See Weiss, "Why Men and Women."

"in order for you to even be considered excellent, you need to be superior, not just excellent."

In this chapter, I want to explore the distinction between men and women. I want us to look at this very complicated issue from the perspective of both male and female. This is critical as it will help us to begin to understand how some male clergy can violate not only their marriage vows but also their clergy vows and think nothing of it, while in the case of most female parishioners it is the very office of pastor and the possibility of a relationship with the "man of God," even if that relationship is secret, that causes some to violate their marriage and Christian values.

Physical Differences between Male and Female

Gender identity is not something that just became vogue in the last 20 or 30 years. All the way back to Genesis chapter 2 we see God in the creation account clearly laying out this distinction between male and female.

> [1]Thus the heavens and the earth and all their array were completed. [2]On the seventh day God completed the work he had been doing; he rested on the seventh day from all the work he had undertaken. [3]God blessed the seventh day and made it holy, because on it he rested from all the work he had done in creation. [4]This is the story of the heavens and the earth at their creation. When the Lord God made the earth and the heavens— [5]there was no field shrub on earth and no grass of the field had sprouted, for the Lord God had sent no rain upon the earth and there was no man to till the ground, [6]but a stream was welling up out of the earth and watering all the surface of the ground— [7]then the Lord God formed the man out of the dust of the ground and blew into his nostrils the breath of life, and the man became a living being.
>
> [8]The Lord God planted a garden in Eden, in the east, and placed there the man whom he had formed. [9]Out of the ground the Lord God made grow every tree that was delightful to look at and good for food, with the

tree of life in the middle of the garden and the tree of the knowledge of good and evil.

[10]A river rises in Eden to water the garden; beyond there it divides and becomes four branches. [11]The name of the first is the Pishon; it is the one that winds through the whole land of Havilah, where there is gold. [12]The gold of that land is good; bdellium and lapis lazuli are also there. [13]The name of the second river is the Gihon; it is the one that winds all through the land of Cush. [14]The name of the third river is the Tigris; it is the one that flows east of Asshur. The fourth river is the Euphrates.

[15]The Lord God then took the man and settled him in the garden of Eden, to cultivate and care for it. [16]The Lord God gave the man this order: You are free to eat from any of the trees of the garden [17]except the tree of knowledge of good and evil. From that tree you shall not eat; when you eat from it you shall die.

[18]The Lord God said: It is not good for the man to be alone. I will make a helper suited to him. [19]So the Lord God formed out of the ground all the wild animals and all the birds of the air, and he brought them to the man to see what he would call them; whatever the man called each living creature was then its name. [20]The man gave names to all the tame animals, all the birds of the air, and all the wild animals; but none proved to be a helper suited to the man.

[21]So the Lord God cast a deep sleep on the man, and while he was asleep, he took out one of his ribs and closed up its place with flesh. [22]The Lord God then built the rib that he had taken from the man into a woman. When he brought her to the man, [23]the man said:

"This one, at last, is bone of my bones and flesh of my flesh; This one shall be called 'woman,' for out of man this one has been taken."

[24]That is why a man leaves his father and mother and clings to his wife, and the two of them become one body.

[25]The man and his wife were both naked, yet they felt no shame.

Difference does not mean inferiority as some have inferred, which cannot be biblically substantiated, but simply difference physically. Both have been called to exercise dominion over the earth,[2] both are coheirs to grace of life, both fell when sin came into the world, and both must be individually redeemed by the blood of the Lamb. Because of their inherent difference, they each have unique roles within the context of the marriage covenant, but this does not mean and should not be extrapolated to mean that one is superior to the other. Like many who have grown up in a conservative theological tradition, I acknowledge that there is a difference between men and women, but these differences in no way establish an inherent inferiority of the woman in relationship to the man. According to Genesis 1, they are coequal partners in God's creation.

Men and Women Are Different Emotionally

Not only are they different physically, men and women are different emotionally. This does not mean that there has not been an influence of culture on the psychosocial development of men and women, however, their biologically inherent differences existed prior to the fall and thus are part of God's design,[3] not something that has taken place because we are in a fallen world. For example, in 1991,

> Diane Halpern, PhD, past president of the American Psychological Association, began writing the first edition of her acclaimed academic text, *Sex Differences in Cognitive Abilities* . . . .
>
> In her preface to the first edition, Halpern wrote: "At the time, it seemed clear to me that any between-sex differences in thinking abilities were due to socialization practices, artifacts and mistakes in the research, and bias and prejudice . . . After reviewing a pile of journal articles that stood several feet high and numerous books and book chapters that dwarfed the stack of journal articles . . . I changed my mind."

2. See Gen 1:26–31.

3. See Gen 1: 27; 2:18–25.

Why? There was too much data pointing to the bio-logical basis of sex-based cognitive differences to ignore, Halpern says. For one thing, the animal research findings resonated with sex-based differences ascribed to people. These findings continue to accrue. In a study of 34 rhesus monkeys, for example, males strongly preferred toys with wheels over plush toys, whereas females found plush toys likable. It would be tough to argue that the monkeys' parents bought them sex-typed toys or that simian society encourages its male offspring to play more with trucks. A much more recent study established that boys and girls nine to 17 months old—an age when children show few if any signs of recognizing either their own or other children's sex—nonetheless show marked differences in their preference for stereotypically male versus stereotypically female toys.[4]

Men and Women Are Different Neurologically

But why are men's and women's brains different? One big reason is that, for much of their lifetimes, women and men have different fuel additives running through their tanks: the sex-steroid hormones. In female mammals, the primary additives are a few members of the set of molecules called estrogens, along with another molecule called progesterone; and in males, testosterone and a few look-alikes collectively deemed androgens. Importantly, males developing normally in utero get hit with a big mid-gestation surge of testosterone, permanently shaping not only their body parts and proportions but also their brains.[5]

Not only can differences between men and women be attributed to neurological, physiological differences; there are also social-cultural influences that have helped to reinforce some of these inherent differences.

4. Goldman, "Two Minds," lines 48–86.
5. Goldman, "Two Minds," lines 188–97.

Men and Women Are Different Socially

Social and cultural norms can significantly influence both the expression of gender identity, and the nature of the interactions between genders.

Differences between "gender cultures" influence the way that people of different genders communicate. These differences begin at childhood. Maltz and Broker's research show that the games children play contribute to socializing children into masculine and feminine cultures. For example, girls playing house promotes personal relationships, and playing house does not necessarily have fixed rules or objectives. Boys, however, tend to play more competitive team sports with different goals and strategies. These differences as children cause women to operate from assumptions about communication, and use rules for communication that differ significantly from those endorsed by most men.

Masculine and feminine cultures and individuals generally differ in how they communicate with others. For example, feminine people tend to self-disclose more often than masculine people, and in more intimate details. Likewise, feminine people tend to communicate more affection, and with greater intimacy and confidence than masculine people. Generally speaking, feminine people communicate more and prioritize communication more than masculine people.

Traditionally, masculine people and feminine people communicate with people of their own gender in different ways. Masculine people form friendships with other masculine people based on common interests, while feminine people build friendships with other feminine people based on mutual support. However, both genders initiate opposite-gender friendships based on the same factors. These factors include proximity, acceptance, effort, communication, common interests, affection and novelty.[6]

6. Boundless, "Gender Differences, lines 1–15.

Deborah Tannen's studies found these gender differences in communication styles (where men more generally refer to masculine people, and women correspondingly refers to feminine people):

> Men tend to talk more than women in public situations, but women tend to talk more than men at home.
>
> Women are more inclined to face each other and make eye contact when talking, while men are more likely to look away from each other.
>
> Men tend to jump from topic to topic, but women tend to talk at length about one topic.
>
> When listening, women make more noises such as "mm-hmm" and "uh-huh", while men are more likely to listen silently.
>
> Women are inclined to express agreement and support, while men are more inclined to debate.[7]

These differences, especially over the last 20 years, have been blurred as we in our society have tried to create a fair and more equitable society for those who traditionally have been marginalized, not only women but also people of color. Out of this right motivation, we have unintentionally, I feel, downplayed the God-ordained distinctions between male and female. This is one reason why the pastor and parishioner need to have appropriate boundaries. Pastors in most settings are esteemed and seen as role models and people to emulate. This puts them in a position not only of power and influence, but also a position of vulnerability. If they do not continue to take care of their own esteem and other needs, including their physical affections needs if married, it is easy to fall into the "messiah syndrome" and think as a pastor that you are even above the things you profess and teach to others.

It is also easy for a well-meaning female parishioner to "project" onto the pastor needs for affirmation and attention that rightly should have been met first by her father within the context of a proper father-daughter relationship and then, as she moves into marriage, by her spouse.

---

7. Boundless, "Gender Differences," lines 36–42.

Sex Is More than an Event; It Is a Relationship

As I write this chapter, I am just coming from a wonderful dinner sponsored by the Moody Bible Institute targeting pastors and their spouses. My dear friend Dr. Crawford Loritts was the speaker. He is the senior pastor of Fellowship Bible Church in Roswell, Georgia, and national speaker for Family Life Marriage Ministry. Dr. Loritts gave a very impactful illustration of speaking to one of his staff in his former ministry, who happened to be a female. She said, "Crawford, I don't feel close to you." In kindness but firmness, Dr. Loritts's response was, "I am glad you do not because that is intentional. I only allow one person to cross certain boundaries in my life, and her name is Karen Loritts."

For those individuals who are in vocational pastoral ministry, allow me to give you five suggestions that I have used down through the years as I have had to navigate the journey vocationally as a pastor who sought to honor my vows to my wife of now forty-one years.

Suggestion 1: Never think you are above a moral failure. As a matter of fact, all of us, even those of us who are pastors, are only one decision away from a fall. Paul in speaking to the church at Corinth said these words: "Therefore let him who thinks he stands take heed that he does not fall" (1 Cor 10:12).

Understand that a fall results when we are not in God's will for us, even if that means we are not doing what God has called us to do, even though we might be in ministry. David the man of God put himself in a place where, as the king of Israel who had led Israel so well, he made a decision outside the will of God that put in him a place where he could not access the grace of God.

> Then it happened in the spring, at the time when kings go out *to battle*, that David sent Joab and his servants with him and all Israel, and they destroyed the sons of Ammon and besieged Rabbah. But David stayed at Jerusalem. Now when evening came David arose from his bed and walked around on the roof of the king's house, and from the roof he saw a woman bathing; and the woman was very beautiful in appearance. So David sent and inquired about the woman. And one said, "Is this not Bathsheba, the daughter of Eliam, the wife of Uriah

53

the Hittite?" David sent messengers and took her, and when she came to him, he lay with her; and when she had purified herself from her uncleanness, she returned to her house. The woman conceived; and she sent and told David, and said, "I am pregnant." (2 Sam 11:1–5)

Here was David, at the pinnacle of his power, doing something stupid because he placed himself in a situation outside of the will of God and therefore was not able to access the power of God that was available to him as a child of God.

Suggestion 2: Maintain spiritual balance in your life. Paul talks about how we need to stand firm against the enemy for the evil day will come. We prepare for that inevitable evil day by putting on the breastplate of righteousness, by taking up the shield of faith, by praying fervently for all the saints, by taking up the sword of the spirit, which is the word of God (Eph 6:14–17). In other words, whether we understand it or not, we are in a spiritual battle, and we can only win when we take up and use those things that God has provided for our protection.

Suggestion 3: No matter what your position, be a person who stays under delegated spiritual authority. Peter would say it like this to the saints in Asia Minor:

> Therefore, I exhort the elders among you, as *your* fellow elder and witness of the sufferings of Christ, and a partaker also of the glory that is to be revealed, shepherd the flock of God among you, exercising oversight not under compulsion, but voluntarily, according to *the will of* God; and not for sordid gain, but with eagerness; nor yet as lording it over those allotted to your charge, but proving to be examples to the flock. And when the Chief Shepherd appears, you will receive the unfading crown of glory. You younger men, likewise, be subject to *your* elders; and all of you, clothe yourselves with humility toward one another, for God is opposed to the proud, but gives grace to the humble.
>
> Therefore humble yourselves under the mighty hand of God, that He may exalt you at the proper time, casting all your anxiety on Him, because He cares for you. Be

of sober *spirit*, be on the alert. Your adversary, the devil, prowls around like a roaring lion, seeking someone to devour. (1 Pet 5:1–8)

Suggestion 4: Prioritize your relationship with your spouse above all relationships. Keep your spouse at the center of your affections. Understand that God, just like he did in the beginning with Adam, knows exactly what you need even better than yourself.

Conclusion

Sex is more than an event; it is a relationship. It is a relationship that is built on mutual understanding, honest communication, and intimacy not just in the bedroom but in life as well. As pastors, one thing that can short-circuit your ministry faster than any bad sermon or bad administrative relationship is the breakdown of the most important relationship outside of your relationship with Christ. Cherish it, for it is indeed a picture for those you lead of Christ's relationship with the church.

Questions for Further Consideration

1. As you read this chapter, what struck you as significant in terms of the differences between women and men? How will this insight influence your ministry?

2. React to the statement: "Men and women are co-equal partners in creation." What are the implications of that statement in terms of how we should treat one another?

3. Dr. Perry mentions four guardrails that can help us maintain sexual purity in our relationships with the opposite sex. Out of the four mentioned, which one will you seek to apply immediately and why? Share this with your spouse or accountability partner so that they can periodically ask you how you are doing in this area.

6

Pornography, the Hidden Evil

Pastor Jim graduated magna cum laude from one of the top evangelical seminaries. His first church was a church plant that grew from five couples to 400 people in less than four years. Immediately his denomination identified him as an up-and-coming leader and recommended him for a larger but plateaued congregation that at one time had 3,000 attendees but had dropped to around 1,500 people as the neighborhood had become much more diverse. Pastor Jim, who was African American, would be the first African American pastor in the history of this well-renowned but declining congregation. Within three years not only had he stopped the decline; he had seen the church grow by 1,000 new members, mostly under 40, with 50 percent being African American and other minority racial groups. So it took the congregation by surprise when on one bright Sunday morning he stood up an announced that he had had an affair, that his wife of 15 years had separated from him, and that he would need to resign.

What happened to this person who was so obviously gifted and called of God? How, in the midst of so much of the evident hand of God, did the enemy come in and destroy not only his ministry but even more importantly his marriage? Well, Pastor Jim had a deep and dark secret that he had not shared with anyone, including his wife: he was and had been since adolescence addicted to pornography. It all started so innocently when he was 13 and had been exposed to a pornographic magazine that his older brother had hidden under his bed. He thought nothing of it at first, being raised in a good Christian home, but six months later while doing some research on the Internet for a term paper that he needed to turn in, he ran across an X-rated site and from that point on he was hooked. After recommitting his life as a high school senior at a young life retreat right before college, he made what would be the first of many vows to God to stop, but somehow, whether it be the stress of school or the stress of his own sense of inadequacy or the stress as a college junior of being convinced of a call to full-time vocational ministry, he would revert back to his secret life of pornography and self-manipulation or masturbation. He would begin to justify this behavior, saying that at least he was not out there like some of his peers having intercourse with another female. And even after he started dating his future wife and then got married, the behavior would subside for a while but would come back up again when he was under significant stress.

The *National Catholic Reporter* editorial staff published an editorial about a report in November 2013 that would rock the church. I have included the accompanying editorial in its entirety as we lay the foundation for what we will be looking at in this chapter. One last disclaimer: by using this editorial, I am not saying that this is a problem only within the Catholic Church, because it is not. It is a problem in other faith traditions as well.

> Thirty-seven percent of male clergy of various faith traditions report Internet pornography as "being a current struggle," and 57 percent of that group report compulsive Internet pornography use, according to a paper, "The Internet and Pornography," delivered during a 2012 symposium on clergy sexual abuse sponsored by the Vatican at the Pontifical Gregorian University in Rome. Representatives of 110 national bishops' conferences and thirty religious orders attended that symposium.
>
> "The most significant signs of this vulnerability are issues related to loneliness and isolation, the lack of self-care, higher expectations of themselves, entitlement, and

lack of education about this aspect of the Internet," the paper said.

The paper notes that research on clergy and pornography use is too scant to make wide generalizations, and that no research on Roman Catholic clergy could be found, but initial impressions from the research that is available support a need for more study and seem "to suggest that clergy in the Roman Catholic Church will need better training and education on this issue."

In July 2011, the Charter for the Protection of Children and Young People, commonly called the Dallas Charter, was updated to include child pornography in its definition of sexual abuse against a minor, a change necessitated by a similar change in canon law. The latest annual audit of diocesan compliance with the Dallas Charter found in the audit period (July 2011 to June 2012) that five clerics were removed from ministry solely because of allegations of possession of child pornography. That was about 2 percent of all allegations, but pornography is involved in a much higher percentage of all cases of sexual abuse of a minor by clergy.

The audit also found that sixteen of the seventy-one dioceses visited by the audit team had not updated their codes of conduct to include child pornography as a prohibited behavior under the updated charter and canon law. The audit team recommended that all diocesan review boards update their policies and procedures to refer explicitly to the possession and/or distribution of child pornography.

We know of three active criminal cases against priests involving child pornography in early November.

All of this makes us want to ask: What were the bishops thinking when they approved the development of a pastoral statement on pornography and its dangerous effects on family life, and never mentioned its dangerous effects on clergy?

Interventions from the floor of the meeting were replete with examples of pornography's pervasiveness and its detrimental effect on family life: increased use of profanity, increased incidents of marital infidelity and divorce, the destruction of trust and intimacy between husbands and wives. There is even a growing number of women viewing it, we were told.

We don't mean to downplay the seriousness of this subject. Pornography and sexual addiction, like any addictive behavior, needs to be dealt with. It can cause damage to intimacy and relationships that calls for spiritual and psychological counseling and support. Its pervasiveness through media has invaded childhoods and coarsened our culture. Vulnerable children and adults—men and women—are exploited and human rights violated by an industry greedy for profits.

There is pastoral work to be done here, without a doubt. But to lay all of this on married men and women with no mention of the clergy, we think the bishops only fool themselves.[1]

The central question of this chapter is this: What are some of the underlying causes of this addiction? Yes, I used the word "addiction" because that is what it is. Secondly, specifically for the pastor, what are some of the consequences of this addiction?

In order to attempt to address this very pervasive and complex question, I have divided the remainder of the chapter into the following sections.

1. What are some of the underlying causes of pornography addiction?

2. As a pastor what are the consequences of this behavior not only on one's ministry but for oneself and one's family?

3. How can a pastor or anyone for that matter begin to experience victory?

1. NCR editorial staff, "Editorial: Don't Ignore Clergy."

What Are Some of the Underlying Causes of Pornography Addiction?

Porn addiction refers to a person becoming emotionally dependent on pornography to the point that it interferes with their daily life, relationships, and ability to function.

This type of addiction may be quite common. Some doctors consider porn addiction to be a hypersexual disorder—an umbrella term that includes behaviors such as excessive masturbation.

A 2019 study suggests that the prevalence of these disorders may be about 3–6 percent. However, the rates have been difficult to determine due to a lack of formal classification . . .

What Is Addiction?

An addiction is more than just an intense interest in something. It is a medical condition that changes the brain and the body and causes a person to feel compelled to continue using a substance or partaking in an activity, even when doing so may cause harm . . .

What the Research Says

A 2017 study of males who sought treatment for problematic pornography use (PPU) found changes in the participants' brains that were consistent with addiction. The researchers found that the brains of the men with PPU reacted differently to erotic images—or the anticipation of them—than the brains of men without PPU.

Use of pornography may also affect people's relationships. For example, some research indicates that pornography creates unrealistic expectations of sex.

A 2013 study found that among heterosexual male participants in couples, the use of pornography was associated with less sexual satisfaction, while the opposite was true for the female participants—pornography was associated with greater sexual satisfaction.

Accessing pornography is easy, and it can require significantly less effort than interacting with a partner. For some, this can contribute to an unhealthy cycle in which porn causes problems in a relationship, leading the person to rely even more heavily on pornography to achieve sexual satisfaction and escape the relationship issues.

Not all research supports the notion that pornography is addictive. A 2014 study emphasizes that many studies of pornography addiction have been poorly designed or biased. The authors caution that little evidence supports a causal relationship between pornography use and its purported harmful effects.[2]

Signs of Pornography Addiction

Even though some in our world system might not think pornography is a problem, as believers we have been exhorted by the apostle Paul to "dwell on these things" which are "true, honorable, right and pure" (Phil 4:8). Pornography is harmful because it contributes to the following results in the life of the person:

- A person's sex life becomes less satisfying.

- Pornography causes relationship issues or makes a person feel less satisfied with their partner.

- A person engages in risky behavior to view pornography, such as doing so at work.

- They ignore other responsibilities in order to view pornography.

- They view progressively more extreme pornography to get the same release that less extreme porn once offered.

- They feel frustrated or ashamed after viewing porn but continue to do so.

- They want to stop using pornography but feel unable to do so.

2. Villines, "What to Know about Porn."

- They spend large sums of money on pornography, possibly at the expense of daily or family necessities.

- They use pornography to cope with sadness, anxiety, insomnia, or other mental health issues.

Causes of Pornography Addiction

At the core of the cause of pornography addiction is the substitution of porn for the life of Christ as the one and ultimate sustainer of one's soul. Because we are fallen people, we tend to seek substitutes for Christ. Unfortunately, a person afflicted by an addiction to pornography, even if they are a believer, might not be willing to share openly and honestly with another person in order to get help, support, and accountability along the way as they seek to address their addiction, due to shame of the addiction. This is even more pervasive for those who are clergy. We are held—and rightly we should be—to a higher standard than those in our congregations,[3] however, even though that is the case, we are still frail, broken human beings who at times, as the song writer says, "are prong to wander."[4]

Even though the ultimate cause for all our addictions is that we are fallen people who live in a fallen world, we might even as clergy need a trained counselor or therapist to help uncover the underlying causes in our soul that have us trapped in such destructive behavior. These vary from person to person and can be uncovered through counseling. Such things as exposure at a young age to pornography, which creates an appetite for even more addictive destructive behaviors that play out as a result of the pornographic addiction, need to be explored carefully by a trained counselor.

3. See Jas 3:1.

4. Robinson and Wyeth, "Come Thou Font of Every Blessing."

What Are the Consequences If a Pastor Struggles with Pornography?

This question is difficult to address definitively, for depending on the church's tradition and theological framework, especially as it relates to Scripture, one can find responses that range from nothing, or acceptance of this behavior as normal, to zero tolerance. What I am about to suggest is based on my understanding of Scripture and over 40 years of vocational ministry, however, it is not the last word on this subject.

Consequence number 1: Loss of credibility within one's marriage. This is not typically listed at the top of the consequence list when discussing this topic, but from my vantage point this is indeed one of the top consequences to marital unfaithfulness. In Matthew 5:27–28 Jesus, when speaking to his disciples, said, "You have heard that it was said, 'You shall not commit adultery';but I say to you that everyone who looks on a woman to lust for her has committed adultery with her already in his heart." Mental infidelity in God's economy is just as dangerous as physical infidelity. For both pull the affections of the husband away from what should be his only and greatest affection above all others except Christ: the marriage, and making sure that the marriage bed is undefiled.[5]

Consequence number 2: Loss of credibility with those they serve. First Timothy 3 is very clear that the elder/overseer (*episkope*)[6] must be above reproach (*anepileptos*).[7] The admonition is written within the context of a local body of believers whom they serve. As a matter of fact, if one were to do an in-depth exegesis on the passage, one would discover that many of the things we think of today in the twenty-first-century Western church are not even addressed in this passage and that the majority of the passage focuses on the elder/overseer's character and family life, not their giftedness and skill.

---

5. See Heb 13:4.
6. Zodhiates, *Hebrew-Greek Key*, 1984.
7. Zodhiates, *Hebrew-Greek Key*, 423.

Consequence number 3: Loss of credibility with a lost and unbelieving world. Matthew 5 talks about how in general we as believers should be salt and light to the world. First Timothy 3:7 talks about how the elder/overseer must be well thought of by outsiders so that he may not fall into disgrace, into the snare of the devil. The recent trend within the last five years of prominent evangelical minsters who have made choices that have hindered their continuing in ministry amplify the real-life consequence of an unbelieving world mocking the church of God because of the unfaithfulness of those who lead the church.

How Can a Pastor Experience Victory?

How can a pastor overcome pornography addiction, and can a pastor be restored to the office of pastor? This is a two-part question.

As it relates to the area of restoration, here are five valuable suggestions that, whether one is a pastor or not, can be helpful:

Suggestion 1: Admit to God your sin and your brokenness. Many of us will at times admit our sin, but it is only when we admit our brokenness can we begin on the road to recovery. John 15:5 says, " I am the vine, you are the branches; he who abides in Me and I in him, he bears much fruit, for apart from Me you can do nothing." Psalm 51:17 says, "A broken and contrite heart, O God, You will not despise." First Peter 5:6 talks about how we need to "humble ourselves under the mighty hand of God." True brokenness, or as some have said, repentance, is the critical first step to the road of deliverance. How can you know if you are truly at a place of brokenness? Well, you will stop blaming others for your sin, you will stop making light of your sin, you will stop exaggerating what you are going to do now that you have fallen for the twentieth time, but you will in meekness and humility come to God and admit how much you need him and how apart from him you truly cannot do anything.

Suggestion 2: Begin to identify what are the triggers in your life that put you in a vulnerable place where the sin becomes more of a comfort to you than the cross. All of us have triggers in our life. In my book, *The Hole in My Soul*, I briefly touch on my relationship with my father and how, when we left the physically abusive home when I was seven, I continually had a hole in my heart (my trigger) that longed to gain approval from other men, so much so that I would be willing to compromise my values for the approval of other men. As I have matured in Christ, even to this day I still have to be very careful that this deep need for approval from people and especially men does not override my desire to gain approval from God.

Suggestion 3: Put a hedge around yourself. Proverbs 7 talks about the young man who lacks sense and who, instead of putting a hedge around himself and not even going near where the temptation was, exposed himself by "passing along the street near her corner, taking the road to her house" (v. 8). The mistake was not in engaging the person who was seeking to tempt the young man; the mistake was in not putting a hedge around himself by not even walking near her street.

Suggestion 4: This requires more than willpower; it requires building accountable relationships, submitting to other men if you are a man or other women if you are a woman.

> Two are better than one, because they have a good reward for their labor. For if either of them falls, the one will lift up his companion. But woe to the one who falls when there is not another to lift him up. Furthermore, if two lie down together they keep warm, but how can one be warm alone? And if one can overpower him who is alone, two can resist him. A cord of three strands is not quickly torn apart. (Eccl 4:9–12)

I can say without a doubt that one of the things that has protected me from myself is having accountable relationships with other men. Last night, prior to writing the first draft of this chapter, my best friend in all the world, Reverend Ben Garrett, called just to see how I am doing especially in the midst of the COVID-19 pandemic. As we reminisced on the phone about our 35-year relationship, it brought joy to my heart just to know that through thick and thin, no matter how bad things have been or might become, Ben will be there for me.

Suggestion 5: Be willing to submit to church discipline. I know the mention of church discipline brings up in many people either memories or experiences that were not God glorifying and even hurtful to people. The Bible does not use church discipline from a framework of something that is punitive, but restorative. "Brethren, even if anyone is caught in any trespass, you who ae spiritual, restore such a one in a spirit of gentleness; each one looking to yourself, so that you too will not be tempted. Bear one another's burdens, and thereby fulfill the law of Christ" (Gal 6:1–2).

> If your brother sins, go and show him your fault in private; if he listens to you, you have won [literally translated " gained"[8]] your brother. But if he does not listen to you, take one or two more with you, so that by the mouth of two or three witnesses every fact may be confirmed. If he refuses to listen to them, tell it to the church; and if he refuses to listen even to the church, let him be to you as a gentile and a tax collector. Truly I say to you, whatever you bind on earth shall have been bound in heaven; and whatever you loose on earth shall have been loosed in heaven. Again, I say to you, that if two of you agree on earth about anything that they may ask, it shall be done for them by My Father who is heaven. For where two or three have gathered together in my name, I am there in their midst. (Matt 18:15–20)

In the case of a pastor/elder, some type of suspension of duties, whether permanent or temporary, depending on the offense, will be warranted. Public trust has been broken; leading others is not something that can be done simply because someone has a position. True leadership only occurs when people willingly follow. In other words, a person can have a position, but that does not mean they are seen as the leader. Those congregations who are part of a network of churches, such as a denomination or association of churches, do have an advantage during times of a moral failure in

---

8. Lexicon, BibleHub.

the pulpit because they can typically call on outside resources from the denomination that will help them with established protocols that have been tested in other settings and can be contextualized for the particular congregation in crisis. Even those movements that function as an association of churches committed to the same doctrinal commitments but do not have direct credential authority, as is the case in many churches from baptistic roots, still can offer to the church upon request outside resources that can help them to navigate the turmoil that will take place once a moral failure has occurred in the pulpit. Some have said that there are different degrees of moral failure. This book does not address this very complex subject, but what it does address, regardless of the type of moral failure, is that every church, based on its theological and historical worldview, needs to have worked through what sins a pastor may be struggling with that are not disqualifying.

The issue of restoration is a little more complicated.

First of all, let me be clear: I believe that, no matter how heinous, God can and does forgive every sin if we come to him seeking forgiveness. First John 1:9 says that if we confess (Greek word *homologeo*)[9] our sin, he is faithful and just to forgive our sin and to cleanse us from all unrighteousness. But Scripture is also clear that for every sin there will be consequences: "Do not be the deceived: God is not mocked, for whatever one sows, that will he also reap" (Gal 6:7; see 6:6–10). James 3:1–2 talks about how we should not desire to be a teacher of the Word, "knowing that as such we will incur a stricter judgment. For we all stumble in many ways, if anyone does not stumble in what he says, he is a perfect [Greek word *teleios*[10]—to complete/mature] man, able to bridle the whole body as well." Going back to the passage in 1 Timothy 3:7, because of the very public nature of the office, those who fall must be restored with the reality in mind that they have not only caused themselves to fall but many others. This is why public rebuke of some sort is always needed in the life of an elder who has fallen. As the servant leader of the flock, the pastor is to help his

9. Zodhiates, *Hebrew-Greek Key*, 3670.
10. Zodhiates, *Hebrew-Greek Key*, 5046.

parishioners by modeling Christ, exhorting them similar to how the apostle Paul did to the saints at Corinth to be imitators of me, just as I also am of Christ" (1 Cor 11:1). The moral failure of an overseer should always have some type of public renouncement of his sin. The circumstance and the church's specific stand on an issue such as pornography will determine if or when the pastor can be restored back into ministry. Five things must take place before restoration should even be considered.

1. Private withdrawal to devote concentrated time with the Lord.

2. Private withdrawal if married to devote contracted time with one's spouse.

3. Private repentance and seeking of forgiveness from anyone whom the pastor might have hurt.

4. Public acknowledgement of the sin and willingness to submit to the decisions of the elders.

5. Rebuilding intimate and accountable relationships with persons of the same sex so that the pastor can be held accountable for not only their past actions but for future endeavors.

Conclusion

Viewing pornography will cause serious problems. Although there are many causes of pornography addiction, treatment will always involve addressing an underlying issue: What have we put in place for our ultimate satisfaction instead of Jesus? This becomes even more complex for the one who is supposed to be providing the care to those who are struggling with pornography, the pastor. Vulnerability, humility, and accountability are keys for anyone seeking to be freed from the chains of pornography, including and especially a person who is a caregiver such as a pastor in this very important area. Be patient with yourself, knowing that God does indeed love you and wants you to live in the freedom he has promised in Christ.

Questions for Further Consideration

1. What are some of the underlying causes of pornography addiction?

2. As a pastor what are the consequences of this behavior not only on one's ministry but for oneself and one's family?

3. How can a pastor (or anyone for that matter) begin to experience victory?

7

The Unique Trauma of
Clergy Sexual Misconduct

PASTORS AND CHURCH LEADERS are often described as shepherds in both the Old and New Testaments. They are to care for, to support, to lead, and to point the flock always to God, who is the ultimate Shepherd. Pastors journey alongside congregants as they navigate the stuff of life: breakups, mental illness, family concerns, abuse. As a pastor, I remember young men and women sharing their most precious hopes, concerns, and fears, trusting me and the other pastors on staff. These were sacred times. Now, as a professor and therapist, I more fully understand how very vulnerable my congregants were, and why sexual abuse, particularly within the church context, is so traumatic. Because pastors represent God, when clergy misconduct occurs, this trauma consequently contributes to spiritual consequences as well.

Within the United States one in three women and one in six men experience some form of non-consensual sexual contact.[1] The offender is usually someone familiar.[2] It is usually a family member, a partner, or a friend. A survey conducted by Baylor

---

1. National Sexual Violence Resource Center, "Statistics," https://www.nsvrc.org/statistics.

2. National Sexual Violence Resource Center, "Statistics," https://www.nsvrc.org/statistics.

University discovered that these offenders include clergy.[3] It defined clergy misconduct as the following: "Ministers, priests, rabbis, or other clergypersons or religious leaders who make sexual advances or propositions to persons in the congregations they serve who are not their spouses or significant others."[4] Here is one of the significant findings from the study:

> In the average American congregation of 400 persons, with women representing, on average, 60 percent of the congregation, there are, an average of 7 women who have experienced clergy sexual misconduct.[5]

Given these numbers, sadly, clergy misconduct is more prevalent than we think.

When I teach my class on trauma for seminarians and counseling students, I ask them to consider the following questions as they assess the impact of various forms of abuse on their parishioners or clients. First, when did the abuse occur? How often did the abuse occur? And finally, who is the offender? Any kind of trauma is detrimental, but studies consistently show that when the trauma is relational and the offender is someone familiar, the impact is particularly distressing.[6] When this familiar person is a parent, a friend, a sibling, or a dating partner or spouse, it is especially devastating. Clergy misconduct involving any form of sexual or emotional intimacy is unique and particularly traumatic because the offender, a pastor, represents God. Pastors are idealized; they are the people that we are taught at a very young age, to trust, to lean on, or to go for support in our time of need. Sexual misconduct is an affront to God, who is the ultimate Shepherd, who always seeks to protect and to guide the flock. Pastors make a promise to God and to their congregation to serve them well and to do no harm. They are trusted and beloved in the community. Therefore, clergy

3. Chaves and Garland, "Prevalence of Clergy Sexual Advances."

4. Chaves and Garland, "Prevalence of Clergy Sexual Advances."

5. Chaves and Garland, "Prevalence of Clergy Sexual Advances."

6. https://www.cdc.gov/injury/features/intimate-partner-violence/index.html.

sexual misconduct violates trust not only with the individual(s), but also with God.

Trauma is often misunderstood as only affecting only one aspect of one's self or life. Renowned psychiatrist Bessel van der Kolk explains the multitudinous effects of trauma, saying,

> Despite the human capacity to survive and adapt, traumatic experiences can alter people's psychological, biological, and social equilibrium to a degree that the memory of one particular event comes to taint all other experiences, spoiling appreciation of the present.[7]

For example, when one has a horrible accident, the focus is often the effect of this event on the body. However, it is not only the body that has been impacted by this traumatic event. Psychologically, the victim may become increasingly anxious and fearful about driving again. They may also fear leaving the house or be concerned about others whom they love going out on the road. Such behaviors inevitably lead to isolation, which creates another set of detrimental consequences of the accident. Thus, this one traumatic event creates a ripple of responses and behaviors that generate potentially destructive behaviors in other areas of one's life. Take, for example, Stan and Ute, a couple who had been in an accident and who were reeling from the impact:

> At home that night, neither Stan nor Ute wanted to go to sleep. They felt that if they let go, they would die. They were irritable, jumpy, and on edge. That night, and for many to come, they drank copious quantities of wine to numb their fear. They could not stop the images that were haunting them or the questions that went on and on: What if they had left earlier? What if they hadn't stopped for gas? After three months of this, they sought help.[8]

Stan and Ute's car accident not only affected their physical selves, it also affected the way they began to engage the world. Prior to seeking help, the accident became the dominant experience

7. Van der Kolk and McFarlane, "Black Hole of Trauma," 4.
8. Van der Kolk, *Body Keeps the Score*, 66.

that dictated their other responses and actions. In fact, victims of trauma are often unconscious of how much their experience has controlled their lives. As van der Kolk observes, "many people may not be aware of the connection between their 'crazy' feelings and reactions and the traumatic events that are being replayed. They have no idea why they respond to some minor irritation as if they were about to be annihilated . . ."[9] Such trauma often reverberates in various domains of one's life. Theologian Shelly Rambo elaborates on the unraveling of trauma in the following:

> Trauma is what does not go away. It persists in symptoms that live on in the body, in the intrusive memories that return. It persists in symptoms that live on in communities, in the layers of past violence that constitute present ways of relating.[10]

This is demonstrated through clergy misconduct. Pastoral theologian Marie M. Fortune defines it as a violation that consists of "sexual comments or suggestions (jokes, innuendos, invitations, and so on), touching, fondling, seduction, kissing, intercourse, molestation, rape, etc."[11] This trauma will inevitably contribute to interpersonal relational difficulties and/or potential mental illness such as post-traumatic stress disorder, anxiety, or depression. Again, any form of harassment and abuse is harmful, but when it is performed by a minister, who is supposed to represent a loving and protecting God, the effects are particularly wounding.

One survivor of childhood clergy abuse describes Father Shanley, the priest who repeatedly abused him, as "the closest thing to God in my neighborhood."[12]

When pastors (for better or worse) are the closest thing to God from a victim's perspective commit acts of abuse, it is not just the pastor causing harm, but God himself instigating their suffering. A pastor holds a lot of power: "power of freedom," "power of

9. Van der Kolk, *Body Keeps the Score*, 66.
10. Rambo, *Spirit and Trauma*, 2.
11. Fortune, *Sexual Violence*, 87.
12. Van der Kolk, *Body Keeps the Score*, 176.

access and accessibility," and "power of knowledge."[13] Unlike therapists, who are required to have supervision in order to maintain their license, pastors are not obligated to do so. Pastors can minister in various settings, and at various times with no real accountability. They also have access to and knowledge of parishioners' personal lives and information. In moments of need, parishioners will divulge secrets, fears, and struggles that others are not privy to. Pastors must acknowledge this power and responsibility, and they must ultimately be accountable to God for the abuse of such powers such as sexual misconduct. Such authority is not given by God and religious institutions to abuse, but rather to serve. Therefore, when a pastor uses their power of freedom, power of access and accessibility, and power of knowledge to sexually abuse congregants, it creates a severe breach of trust.

One of the biggest misconceptions of clergy abuse, or any abuse for that matter, is that the victim could have or should have protected themselves or they "asked for it." However, given the power differential, consent is challenging, as Donald Capps notes here:

> The congregant . . . is by definition vulnerable to the minister or counselor in multiple ways. The person in the former role has fewer resources and less power than the minister or counselor. When the minister or counselor takes advantage of this vulnerability to gain sexual access to another, the minister or counselor violates the mandate to protect the vulnerable from harm . . . meaningful consent to sexual activity requires a context of not only choice but mutuality and equality; hence, meaningful consent requires the absence of fear or the subtle coercion.[14]

Moreover, even if the sexual activity is initiated by the congregant, it is still the minister's responsibility to adhere to the boundaries given their role so that no harm to the congregation ensues as a result of a minister's sexual failure.[15]

---

13. Capps, *Giving Counsel*, 214.

14. Fortune, *Sexual Violence*, 90.

15. Doehring, *Practice of Pastoral Care*, 78.

This abuse also can threaten the relationship that the victim has with God. Thoughts like, "God must not be good or kind after all if my pastor could do this to me" may emerge. Or questions like, "Why did God allow this to happen since a pastor is supposed to help me cultivate my faith?" Thus, the trauma now persists and now lives in their spiritual and communal life:

> Spiritually the consequences are also profound; the psychological pain is magnified and takes on cosmic proportions. Not only is the congregant or client betrayed by one representing God but she or he may also feel betrayed by God and the church . . . this psychological crisis becomes a crisis of faith as well, and the stakes are very high.[16]

Indeed, the stakes are quite high. Some victims leave their church because of the weight of shame they carry. If the sexual misconduct is made public, the victim is often blamed and ostracized, compelling them to leave. Finally, others forsake their faith tradition and God completely. The lack of empathic response from the community is interpreted as God's own rejection and abandonment. Because God is the ultimate Shepherd, when sexual misconduct drives the flock away from the faith and community, that in and of itself is traumatic because what was once an anchor of hope has become a source of suffering.

Context also matters. It is also critical that I engage how sociocultural factors impact trauma such as clergy sexual misconduct. By engaging sociocultural factors, we acknowledge that there is a not a one-size-fits-all to trauma. I can only speak of the Black church since that has been my own experience. The dynamics within a Black church differ from those in other congregations. The Black church is not solely a place of worship but also a haven for many within the Black community. Historically, it is where Black people are emotionally and psychologically nurtured, the church serving as a buffer from the pangs of racism.[17] Therefore, when

16. Fortune, *Sexual Violence*, 89.

17. Lincoln and Mamiya, *The Black Church in the African American Experience*, 1990.

there is sexual misconduct in Black congregations, the trauma is especially salient because the victim's place of shelter is no longer available, or it is now compromised. Womanist pastoral theologian Phillis Sheppard explains that the Black church is a significant cultural self-object that is not exempt from abuse of power, which is especially detrimental to women:

> . . . the Church is an ambivalent cultural institution for many black women, despite the historical role of the black Church as a site group belonging, efficacy, and mental well-being. Black religious experience is not free of sexism, abusive power relationships, or theologies that warp psyche and spirit. Cultural self-objects can serve the mirroring, idealization, and kinship needs of groups, providing a sense of self-continuity—or they can fail to serve them.[18]

Moreover, within the Black church we often refer to pastors as the "mothers and fathers of the church." They are parental figures. Certainly, other churches may also engage such images within their communities. However, within the Black church it is especially salient. Given this dynamic, the experience of clergy misconduct is particularly complex because the pastor not only represents God but may also represent a family member. Therefore, the abuse subconsciously mirrors incest. Studies consistently demonstrate how incestuous relationships are particularly psychologically injurious since those who are supposed to be the most loving and caring (family members) are the initiators of harm.[19] There is much to unpack for the victim so they can move through their healing process, especially when the Black community is hesitant to seek therapeutic services.[20]

One of the many gifts and callings of a pastor, when healthy, is to embody God's deep and unconditional love to others. They should provide insight into the character of God. Unlike many other professions, they are the instrument that God chooses for

18. Sheppard, "Mourning the Loss," 251.
19. Herman, *Trauma and Recovery*, 96–114.
20. Alang, "Mental Health Care among Blacks in America," 346.

healing in various capacities within the church. Therefore, any behavior that taints their pastoral role is so devastating. But when they fully live into their calling, they become a source of healing and comfort.

Before becoming a professor, I served as a counselor at a facility where we treated women who were addicted to various substances. Several themes emerged among my clients: First, many of them had a history of abuse. Second, many of them had a spiritual or religious background that was significant to their formation. Struggling with addiction complicated how they navigated their relationship with God. Many of them were glad to learn that I was also a person of faith, and this created a space for them to share more deeply about their journey with God while attempting to maintain sobriety. For my dissertation, I interviewed Christian women who were survivors of sexual violence. One of the women remembered fondly how her pastor responded to her with love and kindness when she told him of her assault. His response was, "It is not your fault." I asked if her pastor could have said or done anything more for her. She said that statement was enough to comfort her. This pastor played a vital role in her recovery simply by offering this empathic response.

I share these two brief stories to illustrate that spirituality is integral to so many and how critical it is that pastoral leaders care well. Compassion reflects the heart of God, a God who is always on the side of the oppressed and attentive to their cries. One of my favorite verses in the Bible is found in the Old Testament book of the prophet Isaiah. Isaiah says, "Is not this the kind of fasting I have chosen: to loose the chains of injustice and untie the cords of the yoke, to set the oppressed free and break every yoke?" (Isa 58:6 NIV). Although this is not directly to pastors, the truth still stands that one is to see the oppressed free and not cause oppression, especially when you are in ministry. Therefore, when ministers abuse, they desecrate what the victim believes about faith and God. Ministers are to be conduits of God's grace and love—not a deterrent. In this capacity, they can help victims heal.

Conclusion

Sadly, within religious institutions, the experiences of victims of sexual abuse are often minimized or spiritualized. Within the last couple of years, we have learned how often this happens, leaving the victims to fend for themselves. The thought that prayer and time will ameliorate the effects misses the many layers of trauma of sexual misconduct. In the next chapter, I hope to explain why sexual misconduct needs to be addressed for healing, not only for the only individual, but also for the broader church.

Questions for Further Consideration

1. How is trauma different than other forms of suffering?

2. What factors make sexual abuse by clergy particularly harmful?

3. Is it really possible for a congregant to consent to sexual activity with their pastor? Why or why not?

8

Clergy Misconduct and Recovery

So, WHAT DOES RECOVERY from clergy misconduct look like? Recovery must engage the offender, the victim, and the church community. It is also vital that one understands that recovery will take time; there is no way to rush the process of healing, especially when the experience is so traumatic.

When a minister gets ordained and vows to serve God and God's flock, I doubt they enter this vocation desiring to cause harm. Pastors heed the call to ministry because they feel compelled to care and support others. However, along the way the weight of ministry and its responsibilities can begin to affect their pastoral role. Before engaging what recovery might look like for clergy, it is important to consider the factors that might prevent clergy from violating others in the first place.

Though I really enjoyed serving as a pastor, I felt overwhelmed by preaching and constantly caring for others, especially those in crisis. There was simply no keeping up with the daily tasks of ministry. And I only served for three years. In his book *Wounded Healer*,[1] priest Henri Nouwen describes the blessings and challenges of ministry and explains that a pastor's own suffering can be a gift to those they serve. He argues that it is our pain that often ushers us into ministry and enables us to empathize well

1. Nouwen, *The Wounded Healer*, 1979.

with others. My students have their personal reasons for choosing ministry as their vocation. My own story has led me to my profession as a teacher and counselor. It's not coincidental. We are more likely to enter one's anguish when we have experienced such anguish ourselves. Often students find themselves entering ministry and pouring out their lives for others to process or to avoid their own pain.[2] However, when our wounds have not been sufficiently processed and healed before entering ministry, we can cause more harm than good.[3]

Researchers have learned that those in the helping professions especially have these tendencies. "These people who, through their own traumatic experiences, possess a capacity for empathy; however, their need to heal others helps them avoid contact with their own unprocessed trauma."[4] What these ministers eventually discover is that their congregants often exacerbate their wounds. Consequently, this will impact how they care for their congregants. For example, if a pastor has a history of sexual abuse that they have not worked through (ideally in therapy), they may find themselves overidentifying with congregants who share a similar story. It becomes challenging for the pastor to differentiate and detach. This is highly problematic because this is when boundaries become blurred. Another possible response is that pastors may avoid or minimize the victim's experience because they do not want to engage their own history of abuse. This is precisely the reason why I encourage students to process their trauma and work through their struggles prior to delving into ministry. One's history of trauma or mental illness does not preclude one from becoming a minister. It simply means that pastors must acknowledge and recognize how their own story impacts ministry. Therapy is a helpful resource to aid pastors to process their own hurts. Being aware of one's wounds and the possible triggers allows pastors to move forward in the best interests of the victim. Pastors can hold them tenderly, conscious of how their own story may play a role in

2. Pross, "Burnout," 2.
3. Pross, "Burnout," 2.
4. Pross, "Burnout," 2.

providing care. Such awareness enables them to be compassionate and empathic while holding boundaries firmly in place.

I begin with pastors minding their own mental health and story before engaging recovery because these are foundational to caring well for others. When we are aware of our own vulnerability, it helps us to be attentive to our own needs.[5] We recognize that we are human and not the Savior, for that job is already taken by Jesus Christ. Self-awareness thus provides great grounding before embarking upon ministry.

Ministry is demanding. The misconception is that pastors preach on Sunday and that is all their job entails. Yet behind the scenes they are answering crisis calls, dealing with conflict within their congregation, managing a building, and connecting with their community, among other things. They are dealing with their own personal lives and families. If the pastor is the sole pastor and/ or single, that adds another layer of stress because they must carry the burden of ministry alone. It is these various stressors along with the ministerial obligations that often lead to burnout. The fatigue, the lack of support, and the overall loneliness of being in ministry contribute to vulnerability. Studies show that when we are overworked and burned out we are more likely to be susceptible to crossing boundaries.[6] Here is an example from *Giving Counsel: A Minister's Guidebook*, by pastoral theologian Donald Capps, of how a pastor's mental health concerns and lack of support led to a boundary violation:

> The pastor had expressed acute dissatisfaction in his marital relationship and was experiencing anxiety and depression which was noticeable by others with whom he worked and served . . . as weeks progressed Bill admitted that he was involved in a relationship with another woman in his own congregation . . . He described this relationship as intimate but not sexual . . . what Bill did not admit until later in therapy was that the relationship with this female parishioner served his own needs

5. Doehring, *Practice of Pastoral Care*, 73–81.

6. Capps, *Giving Counsel*, 214.

for intimacy and affirmation, which he felt that his wife could not provide.[7]

This example by no means condones clergy misconduct, but it does demonstrate how crucial it is for pastors to nurture themselves and their relationships so as not to seek support from parishioners. It is also important to note that pastors will be attracted to their congregants, and their congregants will be attracted to them at some juncture. However, this does not mean a pastor acts upon the desire. In the therapeutic world this kind of dynamic is called transference and countertransference.[8] Transference is when the parishioner projects onto the pastor their feelings, hopes, and desire, and countertransference is when the pastor projects their feelings, hopes, and desires upon the parishioner.[9] When this happens in a clinical setting, the attraction is simply data. The therapist will wonder what the attraction means and recognize that it is not an invitation for a relationship.[10] Like therapists, when pastors find themselves attracted to congregants it is important for them to engage what the attraction means and to share that information with a colleague or therapist. Capps explains this phenomenon of transference and countertransference well, saying:

> . . . therapists have been taught to recognize the transference/countertransference dynamics discussed earlier in this chapter. Thus, where a minister may take at face value a parishioner's indication that she has "fallen in love" with him, this statement would prompt a psychotherapist to wonder whom he might be "representative of" or a "stand-in" for. Conversely, where a minister might take his own sense of being "in love" with a parishioner face value, the psychotherapist would wonder why he has these feelings toward this woman—"Whom does she represent for me? Who has evoked similar feelings in the past? What fantasies about myself are operating here?"

7. Robison, "Abuse of Power," 4.

8. Capps, *Giving Counsel*, 203.

9. Capps, *Giving Counsel*, 203.

10. Capps, *Giving Counsel*, 221.

Such "wonderings" are not a denial that such feelings are truly felt, but they enable one to gain objectivity on what is occurring and to respond and act more rationally, more calmly . . .[11]

When it comes to sexual attraction to parishioners, I tell my students: "It will happen. It's never about you. Tell someone."

When a pastor has crossed an emotional or sexual boundary with someone within the congregation, it must be addressed. What often happens is that the sexual misconduct is minimized or assumed to have been consensual. As I mentioned in the previous chapter, because of the power differential, it cannot be consensual. The accused pastor must be removed from their position while they are being investigated by church officials, and possibly by the police, depending on the age of the victim. Removal of the clergy member is about protecting the most vulnerable, the one who has been harmed. Pastoral theologian Marie M. Fortune says, "Protection is the community's responsibility. Whether formal (e.g. legal sanctions) or informal (e.g. limits on church activities) steps must be taken to do whatever it is to ensure that the offender does not harm someone again."[12] As we have learned recently in the news, removal of a pastor accused of sexual misconduct is quite challenging, especially when the pastor is beloved by the community. It is hard for parishioners to believe that their pastor could hurt someone. Pastors are often idealized, so to believe that they could sexually harass someone is unimaginable. Therefore, congregants would often rather support their pastor despite evidence so that their own faith in the pastor is not tarnished.

Secondly, the offender must be held accountable for his or her misconduct. I appreciate how Fortune explains why this is necessary for recovery for the offender, victim, and broader church:

> To call an offender to account accomplishes two important steps in healing: (1) it is a stand in solidarity with the victim/survivor, and (2) it is a confrontation with the offender, naming the sin and the consequences of

11. Capps, *Giving Counsel,* 221.
12. Fortune, *Sexual Violence,* 155.

brokenness within the community that resulted in his or her actions. As such calling the offender to account offers the offender the chance to change and to make the brokenness that he or she has caused.[13]

Of course, there are instances where the offender never acknowledges their sin; in those cases, the church community supports the victim with the resources they have and honor what the victim disclosed.[14] However, when the offender does confess and repent of their behavior, consistency of changed behavior will be key. They must show that they are actively engaging in maintaining accountability and getting therapeutic support. Finally, restitution is also evidence of repentance, where the offender provides compensation for the losses he or she has caused.[15]

The process for the offender's recovery will take time and must not be expedited. Again, the victim must be protected from further harm at all costs. This will inevitably cause a fracture within the church system, between those siding with the pastor and others siding with the victim. Regardless of the challenges, the church will endure with the aftermath of clergy misconduct; care of the victim is paramount.

When a congregant informs church leadership of sexual misconduct, it is crucial that they believe their story. I remember years ago a student inquiring about false accusations against pastors. Does this occur? Yes, but it is very rare. The stakes and costs are too high for a person to lie about any form of sexual misconduct. I would rather err on belief and support of the victim than not. And I would be very happy to be wrong in such cases. Victims of clergy sexual misconduct must know that pastoral leadership stands in solidarity with them as they navigate the arduous journey of recovery. Secondly, it is important to empower victims of clergy abuse. Renowned psychiatrist and author of *Trauma and Recovery*, Judith Herman states:

13. Fortune, *Sexual Violence*, 156.
14. Fortune, *Sexual Violence*, 157.
15. Fortune, *Sexual Violence*, 158.

> The first principle of recovery is the empowerment
> of the survivor. She must be the author and arbiter of
> her own recovery. Others may offer advice, support,
> assistance, affection, and care but not cure. Many be-
> nevolent and well-intentioned attempts to assist the
> survivor founder because this fundamental principle
> of empowerment is not observed. No intervention that
> takes power away from the survivor can possibly foster
> her recovery, no matter how much it appears to be in
> her immediate best interest.[16]

Decisions simply cannot be made for victims. They must be asked what they need during every stage of the process of recovery, even when it differs greatly from what the pastoral leadership might assume. A victim of any kind of abuse often feels powerless; therefore, empowering them every step of the way is a means of re-establishing their power.

Victims will also need support as they navigate the spiritual consequences of clergy misconduct. They will undoubtedly have questions for God about the abuse and try to make meaning of it. This requires patience for all parties involved. Some victims may need to take time away from the church to sort out their feelings. It is critical that pastoral leadership not judge or force the victim's process. The best gift that leadership can give the victim is to remind them that they are always welcome if they are ever ready to return. Moreover, it might be helpful for the church to provide additional resources—such as therapy, spiritual directions, or support groups—to support the parishioner. It is essential for the church to stand by the congregant, even if they choose not to remain a part of the church community.

Finally, it is important to be mindful of the role forgiveness plays in recovery for the victim and for the broader church. The tendency may be to engage forgiveness immediately to assuage the ramifications of the sexual misconduct. However, when there is a haste to forgive the offender there is not much room to grieve

---

16. Herman, *Trauma and Recovery*, 134.

the sin of sexual misconduct.[17] It important for the congregation and victim to acknowledge the grievance and not feel compelled to forgive the offender without sufficiently mourning their pain and suffering.[18] This is especially important for the victim. They get to choose when they forgive. This is also a critical component of empowering victims, as Fortune explains:

> The choice on the part of the survivor to let go only happens when she or he is ready to let go. When the healing is enough and the survivor feels safe and strong enough, she or he will be ready to let go and can make that choice. Even then, letting go is not easy. God's grace, which is known through prayer and the presence of the Holy Spirit, can empower a survivor to forgive.[19]

Forgiveness is indeed both a theologically and psychologically important part of healing, but always at the pace and readiness of the one who is suffering. For those who journey with the victim, we trust not only their process but the God who is the source of healing and compassion to guide them along the way.

We have looked at the recovery process for the offender and the victim after sexual misconduct. Now it is important to briefly engage what recovery might look like for a congregation. When a pastor has been accused of sexual misconduct and removed, the entire congregation suffers. Feelings of anger, grief, fear, and overwhelming loss will inevitably ensue. How could their pastor do such a thing? Did they really do it? How could have they missed it? What will happen to our church community now? Depending on a parishioner's own abuse history, clergy sexual misconduct can trigger their own story of betrayal. Similarly, to begin the recovery process for the offender and victim, there must be acknowledgment of what happened. To minimize or to deny the impact of this grievance will only exacerbate the pain of the congregation. Therefore, informing the congregation of the steps that have been taken (focusing on the pertinent information) to assure that no one else

17. Herman, *Trauma and Recovery*, 188-189.

18. Herman, *Trauma and Recovery*, 188-189.

19. Fortune, *Sexual Violence*, 164.

has been harmed is important.[20] Providing referrals for mental health services is another important aspect of good congregational care.[21] Based on the size of the congregation, listening and praying sessions for those who need to engage their spiritual practices in community will also be vital. Finally, the church is blessed with rituals.[22] A service or services of lament where the community can mourn together and comfort each other can be a significant way to process the suffering. Planning such services will take time and creativity, but it is imperative that leadership make every effort assist the congregation with their process.

Conclusion

According to theologian Shelly Rambo, "The experience of traumatic suffering is intensified by the invisibility and unspeakable nature of violence. A witnessing presence in trauma will make visible what is rendered invisible. If a person who survives trauma can put words to that experience, the process of healing can take place."[23] Clergy misconduct is often an invisible trauma in our churches because it is too painful and fearful for both the victim and the leadership to disclose. For the victim, the pain and fear often entail shame and fear of how the rest of the community will respond. For the leadership, it is about how this disclosure will affect the broader church and community. When these concerns arise, it is vital to remember God's nature as a God who is for the hurting and the oppressed. Victims of clergy misconduct are those suffering in our midst. To remain silent does not reflect a God who sets captives free. Therefore, we must make the invisible visible so that our all-loving and compassionate God is revealed to victims, reminding them they are seen and known so healing can take place.

20. Fortune, *Sexual Violence*, 124–61.

21. Fortune, *Sexual Violence*, 124–61.

22. https://www.faithtrustinstitute.org/resources/liturgy

23. Rambo, *Spirit and Trauma*, 123.

Questions for Further Consideration

1. Why is it important that pastors receive help for their own traumas?

2. What steps should be taken to bring restoration to a pastor when sexual misconduct occurs?

3. What actions help a victim of clergy sexual abuse to recover? What actions hinder that recovery?

4. What steps can be taken to bring healing to a congregation when clergy sexual misconduct occurs?

9

Concluding Thoughts

WE BEGAN THIS BOOK with the unfortunate and sad story of Reverend Bill Hybels and the demise of someone whose ministry continues to impact millions around the world in spite of his alleged moral failure. As I reflect on this unfortunate story, I do not, and I do not want you to, have any hint of condemnation or judgment. As a matter of fact, the thought that continues to go through my mind and heart is simply this: *There, but for the grace of God, go I.*

As we conclude this book, Dr. Pierre and myself want to offer to those who read our book a glimmer of hope by looking at the story of Peter.

If you are a preacher, or even if you are not, I am sure you are familiar with the story of the impulsive young leader Peter. John 13 begins the story of what we have come to call the Lord's Supper. It is the night before Jesus would be crucified, and he gives to his disciples a new command to love one another just as he has loved them. Why? For it is by their love that the world will know that they are his disciples—if they love one another (vv. 34–35). We see Peter for the second time[1] interjecting himself into the conversation, by saying, in response to Jesus' statement that it was time for the Son of Man to be glorified and go to His Father (vv. 31–33),

1. The first time is when he told Jesus what to do and that he did not want Jesus to wash his feet.

"Lord, where are your going?" Then Peter asked, "Lord, why can I not follow You right now? I will lay down my life for you." Jesus replied, "Will you lay down your life for Me? Truly, truly, I say to you, a rooster will not crow until you deny Me three times" (vv. 36–38).

Now, I don't know about you, but if I were Peter, I would have been scratching my head. *What is Jesus talking about? Doesn't he know how much I love him? Doesn't he know how loyal I am to him? Doesn't he know I will never betray him?* But yet even though he sincerely felt that, just like many of us have also felt that, we also need to realize, as the apostle Paul would say in Ephesians, that "our struggle is not against flesh and blood but against the rulers, against the authorities, against the cosmic powers of darkness, against evil, spiritual forces" (6:10–12). Or as Peter himself would say many years later in 1 Peter 5:8, we need to "be of sober spirit, be on the alert. Your adversary the devil, prowls around like a roaring lion seeking someone to devour." Why? Because as Jeremiah says, "The heart is more deceitful than all else, and is desperately sick—who can understand it?" (Jer 17:9).

As a result, Peter would find himself a few hours later denying the very God he had sworn allegiance to. Our point is simply this: "even the best of us" are susceptible to turn our back on our vows to God, our families, and our congregations if we do not continue to do the work we need to do to be vigilant against the schemes of the enemy.

Conclusion

This is the point of this book, or as I (Dwight) would say in my homiletics classes, the "big idea." All of us, especially and even if you have accepted a call to represent Christ as one of his shepherds, are susceptible to fall prey to sexual failure. May we everyday wake up with a holy reverence for our great God and a holy awareness of our own frailty and thus a holy need to continually come before the one "who is able to keep you from stumbling, and to make you stand in the presence of His glory blameless with great joy, to the only God our Savior, through Jesus Christ our Lord, be glory, majesty, dominion and authority, before all time and now and for-ever. Amen" (Jude 1:24–25).

Question for Further Consideration

Discuss with your spouse, pastor or accountability partner the big idea of the book. "All of us, including (and especially) pastors, are susceptible to fall prey to sexual failure." What one takeaway will you commit to working on as a result of this book? Share this with either your spouse, pastor, or accountability partner, and develop a plan of implementation.

"May the God of peace Himself sanctify you entirely; and may your spirit and soul and body be preserved complete, with-out blame at the coming of our Lord Jesus Christ." 1 Thess. 5:23. Shalom!

Bibliography

Alang, Sirry M. "Mental Health among Blacks in America: Confronting Racism and Constructing Solutions," Health Services Research 54(2) (April2019), 346-355. DOI: 10.1111/1475-6773.13115

Bandura, Albert. *Social Learning Theory*. Englewood Cliffs, NJ: Prentice Hall, 1977.

Bergeron, Pierre. "The Compulsive Leader." February 26, 2015. http://www.sisleadership.com/the-compulsive-leader/.

————. "The Narcissistic Leader." December 5, 2017. http://www.sisleadership.com/the-narcissistic-leader-2/.

————. "The Paranoid Leader." March 12, 2015. https://www.sisleadership.com/the-paranoid-leader/.

————. "The Passive Aggressive Leader." April 2015. http://www.sisleadership.com/the-passive-agressive-leader/.

Boundless. "Gender Differences in Social Interaction." *Sociology—Cochise College Boundless.* May 26, 2016. https://www.boundless.com/users/493555/textbooks/sociology-cochise-college/gender-stratification-and-inequality-11/gender-and-socialization-86/gender-differences-in-social-interaction-502–10212/.

Bowlby, John. "The Nature of the Child's Tie to His Mother." *International Journal of Psychoanalysis* 39.5 (1958) 350–73.

Callahan, Kennon. *Twelve Keys to an Effective Church: Strategic Planning for Mission.* San Francisco: Harper and Row, 1983.

Capps, Donald. *Giving Counsel: A Minister's Guidebook.* St. Louis: Chalice, 2001.

Centers for Disease Control and Prevention. "Prevent Domestic Violence in Your Community." https://www.cdc.gov/injury/features/intimate-partner-violence/index.html.

Chaves, Mark, and Diana Garland. "The Prevalence of Clergy Sexual Advances towards Adults in Their Congregations." *Journal for the Scientific Study of Religion* 48.4 (2009) 817–24.

Cherry, Kendra. "The Purpose of Our Emotions: How Are Feelings Help Us Survive and Thrive." *Verywell Mind,* May 17, 2020. https://www.verywellmind.com/the-purpose-of-emotions-2795181.

Bibliography

Doehring, Carrie. *The Practice of Pastoral Care: A Postmodern Approach.* Louisville: Westminster John Knox, 2015.

Eisenberg, N., and A. S. Morris. "Children's Emotion-Related Regulation." Advances in Child Development and Behavior 30 (2002) 189–229.

FaithTrust Institute. "#MeToo #ChurchToo." https://www.faithtrustinstitute.org/churchtoo.

Flynn, Kathryn A. *The Sexual Abuse of Women by Members of the Clergy.* Jefferson, NC: McFarland, 2003.

Forte, Tiago. "The Body Keeps the Score: Brain, Mind, and Body in the Treatment of Trauma (Book Summary)." *Forte Labs* blog, October 22, 2019. https://fortelabs.co/blog/the-body-keeps-the-score-summary/.

Fortune, Marie. *Is Nothing Sacred?: When Sex Invades the Pastoral Relationship.* San Francisco: HarperCollins, 1989.

———. *Sexual Violence: The Sin Revisited.* Cleveland: Fortress, 2005.

Fowler, James W. *Stages of Faith: The Psychology of Human Development and the Quest for Meaning.* New York: Viking, 1981.

Goldman, Bruce. "Two Minds: The Cognitive Difference between Men and Women." *Stanford Medicine*, Spring 2017. https://stanmed.stanford.edu/2017spring/how-mens-and-womens-brains-are-different.html.

Halpern, Diane F. *Sex Differences in Cognitive Abilities.* New York: Psychology, 2012.

Herman, Judith. *Trauma and Recovery: The Aftermath of Violence—From Domestic Abuse to Political Terror.* Rev. ed. New York: Basic Books, 1997.

Heggen, Carolyn Holderread. "Sexual Abuse by Church Leaders and Healing for Victims." *Mennonite Quarterly Review* 89 (January 2015) 81–93.

Hybels, Lynne, and Bill Hybels. *Rediscovering Church: The Story and Vision of Willow Creek Community Church.* Grand Rapids: Zondervan, 1995.

"James Fowler's Stages of Faith." Psychology Charts. http://psychologycharts.com/james-fowler-stages-of-faith.html.

Koster, Steven. "Why Pastors Have Affairs: Sacred Boundaries and Sexual Abuse." *Family Fire*, March 30, 2017. https://familyfire.reframemedia.com/articles/Why-pastors-have-affairs.

Krejcir, Richard. "Focus on the Family Statistics on Pastors." http://www.intothyword.org/apps/articles/?articleid=36562.

Lassar, Mark. "Sexual Addition and Clergy." *Pastoral Psychology* 39.4 (1991).

Lee, Morgan. "Here's How 770 Pastors Describe Their Struggle with Porn." *Christianity Today*, News & Reporting, January 26, 2016. https://www.christianitytoday.com/news/2016/january/how-pastors-struggle-porn-phenomenon-josh-mcdowell-barna.html.

Lincoln, C. Eric & Lawrence H. Mamiya. *The Black Church in the African American Experience.* Durham, NC: Duke University Press, 1990.

Martinez, Jessica. "5 Reasons Ministers Are More Vulnerable to Sexual Temptation." *Christian Post*, October 4, 2014. https://www.christianpost.com/news/ex-porn-addict-and-minister-5-reasons-pastors-are-more-vulnerable-to-sexual-temptation.html.

Bibliography

McDowell, Josh. *The Porn Phenomenon: The Impact of Pornography in the Digital Age*. Ventura, CA: Barna Research Group, 2016.

McIntosh, Gary, and Samuel Rima. *Overcoming the Dark Side of Leadership: How to Become an Effective Leader by Confronting Potential Failures*. Grand Rapids: Baker, 2007.

McLeod, Saul. "Attachment Theory." *Simple Psychology*, February 5, 2017. https://www.simplypsychology.org/attachment.html.

Means, Patrick. *Men's Secret Wars*. Grand Rapids: Baker, 2006.

Mills, Bill, and Craig Parro. *Finishing Well in Life and Ministry: God's Protection from Burnout*. Palos Heights, IL: Leadership Resources International, 1997.

Morris, Amanda Sheffield, et al. "The Role of the Family Context in the Development of Emotional Regulation." *Social Development* 16.2 (May 2007) 361–88.

National Sexual Violence Resource Center. "Statistics." https://www.nsvrc.org/statistics.

NCR editorial staff. "Editorial: Don't Ignore Clergy in Effects of Pornography." *National Catholic Reporter*, November 21, 2013. https://www.ncronline.org/news/parish/editorial-dont-ignore-clergy-effects-pornography.

Nouwen, Henri. *The Wounded Healer: Ministry in Contemporary Society*. New York: Image, 1972.

Perry, Dwight. *The Hole in My Soul*. Self-published through Createspace, 2013.

Plass, Richard, and James Cofield. *The Relational Soul: Moving from False Self to Deep Connection*. Downers Grove, IL: InterVarsity, 2014.

Pross, Christian. "Burnout, Vicarious Traumatization and Its Prevention." *Torture* 16.1 (2006) 1–9.

Rainer, Thomas S. "Eight of the Most Significant Struggles Pastors Face." *Church Answers* blog, March 1, 2014. https://churchanswers.com/blog/eight-of-the-most-significant-struggles-pastors-face/.

Rambo, Shelly. *Spirit and Trauma: A Theology of Remaining*. Louisville: Westminster John Knox, 2010.

Robison, Lisa Hansen. "Abuse of Power: A View of Sexual Misconduct in a Systemic Approach to Pastoral Care." *Pastoral Psychology* 52.5 (May 2004) 395–404.

Rutter, Peter. *Sex and the Forbidden Zone: When Men in Power—Therapists, Doctors, Clergy, Teachers, and Others—Betray Women's Trust*. Los Angeles: Tarcher, 1989.

Schaffer, H. Rudolph, and Peggy E. Emerson. "The Development of Social Attachments in Infancy." *Monographs of the Society for Research in Child Development* 29.3 (1964) 1–77.

Sheppard, Phillis. "Mourning the Loss of Cultural Selfobjects: Black Embodiment and Religious Experience after Trauma." *Practical Theology* 1.2 (2008) 233–57.

Simon, George. "Functional Narcissism and Culture." Blog, January 19, 2018. https://www.drgeorgesimon.com/functional-narcissism-and-culture/.

Bibliography

Strauch, Alexander. *Biblical Eldership: An Urgent Call to Restore Biblical Church Leadership.* Littleton, CO: Lewis & Roth, 1995.

Thoburn, J. W., and J. O. Balswick. "Demographic Data on Extra-Marital Sexual Behavior in the Ministry." *Pastoral Psychology* 46.6 (1998) 447–57.

Thomas, Robert L., ed. *New American Standard Exhaustive Concordance of the Bible: Hebrew-Aramaic and Greek dictionaries.* Nashville: Holman, 1981.

Van der Kolk, Bessel. *The Body Keeps the Score: Brain, Mind, and Body in the Healing of Trauma.* New York: Penguin, 2015.

Van der Kolk, Bessel A., and Alexander C. McFarlane. "The Black Hole of Trauma." In *Traumatic Stress: The Effect of Overwhelming Experience on Mind, Body, and Society,* edited by Bessel A. Van der Kolk, Alexander C. McFarlane, and Lars Weisaeth, 3–23. New York: Guilford, 1996.

Villines, Zawn. "What to Know about Porn Addiction." *Medical News Today,* January 29, 2020. https://www.medicalnewstoday.com/articles/porn-addiction.

Weese, Carolyn, and J. Russell Crabtree. *The Elephant in the Boardroom: Speaking the Unspoken about Pastoral Transitions.* San Francisco: Jossey-Bass, 2004.

Weiss, Robert. "Why Men and Women See Infidelity So Differently." *Psychology Today* blog, *Love and Sex in the Digital Age,* July 10, 2017. https://www.psychologytoday.com/us/blog/love-and-sex-in-the-digital-age/201707/why-men-and-women-see-infidelity-so-differently.

Zodhiates, Spiros, ed. *The Complete Word Study Dictionary: New Testament.* Nashville: AMG, 1992.

———. *The Hebrew-Greek Key Study Bible.* Grand Rapids: Baker, 1984.